Prenatally Exposed Kids In School

*What to Do
How to Do It*

(Formerly *"Crack Kids" in School*)

Danni Odom-Winn
Dianne Dunagan

EDUCATIONAL ACTIVITIES, INC.
Box 392
Freeport, NY 11520

©1991 Activity Records, Inc.
All rights reserved.
No part of this book (except the forms) may be duplicated in any way
without the written permission of Educational Activities, Inc.

Printed in the United States
B 302
ISBN # 0-7925-1867-5
Library of Congress #91-77184

ACKNOWLEDGMENTS

To Bob Middlemiss…for telling the publisher what we do.

To Al and Norma Harris for listening to our thoughts
and believing we could put them on paper.

…and especially to Leon Dunagan for taking our jumbled rhetoric
and creating beautiful forms.

AND SPECIAL THANKS TO…

Toni Barnett
Bobbie Dean
Buddy Dunn
Rose Falco
Teri Kirkland
Terri Roberson

CREDITS

Senior Editor: Rosalie Dow
Editor: J. Lynne Dodson
Book Design: Rachel Janner
Cover Design: Norma Harris
Photography: Avalon Studios
Color Separations: Profile
Printed by: Port City Press, Inc.

Table of Contents

Foreword i

Preface 1

Chapter 1 Where Does the Square Peg Fit?...............................4
  A. Explanation and Instructions for
     Completing the PDD Characteristics Checklist.........................5
  B. Completed Sample of the PDD Checklist 7
  C. Explanation and Instructions for Completing the
     Communication/Behavior Prompts Form...............................9
  D. Completed Sample of the Communication/
     Behavior Prompts Form...11
  E. Explanation and Instructions for Completing the
     Developmental Ages Checklist 13
  F. Ready, Set, Begin!...19

Chapter 2 Room Set Up 21
  A. What to Do When…...21
  B. Materials: The Dream and Reality.......................................23

Chapter 3 Getting Control..31
  A. Sitting Down (In-Seat Behaviors) 33
  B. Staying Down (Waiting) 35
  C. Looking Up (Attending) 37
  D. Strike Out (Aggressive Behavior) 41
  E. Changing the Tune (Self Stimulating
     Behaviors)...43
  F. Let's Play School (Age Appropriate School
     Behaviors)...45

**Chapter 4 Communicating Means More Than
Talking** 50
  A. Talk It Up! (Language Acquisition) 52
  B. Let's Make a Connection (Brain Language)..........................54
  C. Too Much…Too Little Talk (Teacher-Talk) 58
  D. Using Our Hands (Sign Language) 60

Chapter 5 Classroom Communication Lightbulbs...................75
   A. Can You Hear Me? (Auditory) 76
   B. I See You (Visual)..79
   C. Touch Me! (Tactile) 84
   D. That Smells Funny! (Smell) 85
   E. It Tastes Yukky! (Taste) 86
   F. What ya gonna do? (Themes)......................................87

Chapter 6 Parents are People, Too....................................89
   A. Caretaker/Parent Interview Guide 89
   B. Dealing with Parents' Frustration First 92
   C. Promoting a Buy-In 93

Chapter 7 Hodgepodge..95
   A. Bandages (Classroom Management Tips).................95
   B. Lollipops and Rainbows (Reinforcers).....................100
   C. Collecting Data 102
   D. Etcetera 106

Forms and Checklists..108
   A. PDD Characteristics Checklist 108
     (This form is also included on the second page of
     the Developmental Ages Checklist, page 112)
   B. Communication/Behavior Prompts 109
   C. Developmental Ages Checklist 110
   D. Caretaker/Parent Interview Guide 113
   E. Composite Behavior Form...114
   F. Behavior Frequency Form 115

References..116

Index..119

Foreword

This book was written by teachers who have taught sets of autistic twins, a child who talks to Donald Duck, many children who bite and have daily tantrums, and children who come to school with no behavioral prerequisites for learning in the classroom. The book was written for teachers who know the frustration of attempting to teach children who have been emotionally and physically scarred before they entered school for the first time.

Social predictions for the 1990s reveal that we can expect more addicted children, more socially maladjusted children, and more students who are at high risk for academic failure than at any time in American history. Educators will still be expected to teach manners and morals along with basic skills. Schools will not be able to correct all the problems in our society. However, teachers can repair some of the problem behaviors exhibited by children in the classroom by using specific strategies described in this manual.

The techniques for facilitating improvement in behavior and communication come from educators who have experimented with the latest educational fads and the oldest textbook scenarios. They have extracted simple and reliable methods that truly do seem to modify the child's behavior without the use of physical punishment. They have encouraged the child to make better choices in an atmosphere of acceptance and love. When the child can communicate more effectively with you and his or her classmates, you will be amazed at the change in attitude. You will become an agent for child change if you will try these suggestions in your classroom.

Dorothy F. Sutherland, Ed. D.
CCC-SLP Associate Professor of Communicative Disorders.
Columbia College, Columbia, SC.

Preface

Pervasively Developmentally Delayed children are globally delayed in some, if not all, developmental areas (behavioral, physical/motor, communication, and intellectual). For instance, a child experiencing global delays in communication will generally have difficulty in behavior, interpersonal skills, and academics. Each area of delay impacts on the others. A child with academic delays will most likely experience difficulty in behavior, socialization, and progress in school.

Children prenatally exposed to drugs experience delays in many areas; few of these children are unaffected. We believe that the MAJORITY of "crack" children are pervasively developmentally delayed. Early identification increases the chances of mainstreaming to regular classrooms at a younger age.

Many words come to mind when we think about educating, socializing, and making contact with PDD children: desperate, horrified, afraid, running scared, or just plain running. PDD children are now coming to school labeled as crack kids, prenatally drug exposed, Fetal Alcohol Syndrome children, autistic, hyperactive, Asperberger Syndrome, other health impaired, attention deficit disorder (ADD) or attention deficit disorder with hyperactivity (ADHD), and childhood aphasics, to mention a few.

This book is written by educators for educators. It is not a theoretical tome, nor is it a philosophical book delving into the psyche of these special children. It is, we hope, a practical "first aid" manual for educators who find themselves face to face with a PDD child in the classroom.

We have written from our experience: twenty-six years for one author and seventeen for the other. We have taught, fought, cried, laughed, and shouted "hallelujah" together over PDD children. We have seen regression, progress, minute steps, giant steps, hysterical parents, teachers, administrators, and students. We have seen PDD children conquer mountains as well as ant hills and we've also watched those same kinds of children apparently regress, leaving student and teacher the task of climbing that mountain or hill again.

You have probably heard about or seen these children in special education classes where they exhibit nonverbal, oppositional behaviors. Many of them don't react to anything any time. They also sit in regular classrooms. Maybe even yours.

These children are:
- Unable to attend for more than 10-30 seconds
- Disorganized
- Hyperactive
- Aggressive
- Angry all the time

Do these behaviors sound familiar to you?

These characteristics are also prevalent in varying degrees in crack kids. Remember that PDD children do not necessarily exhibit all these characteristics:

1. PDD children are runners! Skinned knees, broken bones, bloody noses, and sprained ankles on staff members who race to keep up with them all attest to that.

2. PDD children's instincts are often primitive and sometimes irrational. They fear light, dark, thunder, other children, you, chairs, orange juice—the list is endless. Treat these children with as much respect as you give the warning signals at a railroad crossing.

3. They are not able to communicate their anxieties to you. They may fidget, cry, or sit absolutely still in the midst of the worst thunderstorm you have ever seen. This does not mean that they are not feeling anything. They may be scared to death, but they simply lack the requisite skills to communicate that fear to you.

4. Their academic performances range from one to five years below their peers in reading comprehension and math. Both fine- and gross-motor skills are poor. Writing is generally a laborious task for them, and their work is illegible.

5. They look as if they have been put together by committee. Nothing fits. Everything about them appears out of sync. Walking, talking, running, and even eating are monumental tasks for many crack kids. Their fine-motor skills may not be age-appropriate, and they can do little with the usual finesse of the young. They may have a beautiful face, a slender body, and grossly misshapen hands. The differences in other PDD children may be more subtle: They get dirty, fall, hurt themselves, or break something just moving from their classroom to the cafeteria.

6. They have trouble getting along with anyone. They don't understand the "how to's" of conversations or playing, for instance, turn-taking and sharing.

7. When they get older, they deny they have broken the rules because they don't know the rules, or even what "breaking the rules" means. If these children know the rules by rote, they still don't follow the rules because they don't understand them; or worse, they don't understand that the rules apply to them. They may show no remorse for any wrongdoing.

Perhaps the very best example of how PDD children think is a very common one for us. It took over eight months to teach a small group (six children, ages eight to ten years) to stop at the stop sign outside our building. Their teachers did it with persistence, repetition, blood, sweat, and tears! That was nearly two years ago. Since then, not one person has been able to successfully teach any of those children when it is safe to go. Think about that! The language and vocabulary concepts they would have to understand before learning to *go* include the words *don't, go, until, road,* and *clear,* not to mention an understanding of the action of *go* and *is coming*. You would have to concretely name every color car; then move to trucks, jeeps, buses, eighteen wheelers, motorcycles, bicycles, vans, trash trucks, tankers, and every other vehicle. Can you imagine the amount of time needed to teach this one safety concept? The difficulty in teaching this concept lies in PDD children's inability to think abstractly. Their processing skills are limited and in some cases nonexistent. They usually perceive only the most concrete ideas.

We believe that if you set about educating these children methodically, in a well-organized fashion, and sprinkle their school lives with love, compassion, and firmness, they can reach their maximum potential.

As you begin your journey along the yellow brick road of educating PDD children, remember that without the concrete holding the bricks together, your trip would be a bumpy one.

GOOD LUCK!

> *We believe that if you set about educating these children methodically, in a well-organized fashion, and sprinkle their school lives with love, compassion, and firmness, they can reach their maximum potential.*

1 Where Does the Square Peg Fit?

The first week of school has come and gone. You have gotten your students settled in and have faced the unalterable fact that one or more of them is different...really different. In truth, that child's behavior is bizarre, either nearly uncontrollable or so withdrawn that ice cream doesn't draw a response.

You are going to need to know some basic information about the monumental task we are now facing in education as the problem of illicit drug usage by expectant mothers has grown in our society. For years, the unborn have been exposed to marijuana, cocaine, PCP, barbiturates, alcohol, angel dust, amphetamines, and a plethora of other drugs. The newest enemy of the fetus is crack, a pure form of cocaine. Crack is a light brown or milky white pellet (rock) which is usually smoked. Crack is not just a street drug; it is also found in the upper crust of society and all the layers in between. Jet setters as well as the homeless fly high on this drug.

Statistics say that one of every ten newborns in the United States is exposed in the womb to one or more drugs. Some of these kids have severe physical abnormalities, but the majority look just like all other sweet-faced kids. The differences are usually more subtle, and as the children get older these differences are manifested in major social/behavioral problems and learning difficulties.

In the fetus, crack causes blood vessels to constrict, which in turn causes a loss of oxygen and nutrients. The cocaine also alters brain neurotransmitters, which carry information from nerve cell to nerve cell. Many of the child's behavioral difficulties, impulsivity, and moodiness can be related directly to central nervous system damage caused by the drug.

Children born to drug-addicted mothers (and/or fathers) aren't the only pervasively developmentally delayed (PDD) children encountered in today's classrooms. Children suffering from Fetal Alcohol Syndrome, autism, hyperactivity, Asperberger Syndrome, and aphasia share the PDD challenges.

You have heard the bad news; there is some good news and you are part of that. You can acquire the skills needed to help these square pegs fit into society's round holes.

You have heard the bad news; there is some good news and you are part of that. You can acquire the skills needed to help these square pegs fit into society's round holes.

A. Explanation and Instructions for Completing the PDD CHARACTERISTICS Checklist

Early identification and intervention are critical to successfully educate PDD children. These children, regardless of their diagnostic label, share many basic characteristics and should be treated in a similar fashion, educationally. These characteristics have been categorized on the **Pervasively Developmentally Delayed Characteristics (PDD) Checklist** under four headings: communication, physical/motor, behavior, and intellectual. Even though we have placed these characteristics under specific headings, they are not written in stone. Many traits "bleed" into several categories.

Look over the list and check all characteristics that apply to the child you are evaluating. Try to get input from all involved with the child: school counselor, physical education teacher, music teacher, art teacher, librarian, speech/language specialist, occupational therapist, physical therapist, special education teacher, school psychologist, nurse, and the parent/guardian.

Use these explanations to help you fill out the **Pervasively Developmentally Delayed Characteristics Checklist** at the back of the book.

Early identification and intervention are critical to successfully educate PDD children.

Communication

1. Inappropriately expresses needs (cries/tantrums instead of reaching, pointing, or speaking, etc.)
2. Makes little eye contact (fleeting glances in the direction of your face)
3. Makes unusual sounds when distressed or even happy (guttural, peeps, etc.)
4. Rarely smiles; almost never laughs (solemn)
5. Lacks facial expression (flat affect)
6. Relates poorly to people (in "own world," poor peer interaction)
7. Unintelligible. Has mild to severe articulation problems
8. Makes limited verbal responses (short utterances or no speech)
9. Displays echolalic behavior (repeats words, phrases out of context)
10. Speaks with abnormal voice (pitch too high/low; too loud/soft; no inflection)
11. Responds off topic (off-the-wall answers to questions)

Physical/Motor

1. Exhibits multiple health problems such as: disproportioned head/body extremities ratio, vision and hearing problems, facial abnormalities, allergies, heart defects, tremors (seizures), breathing difficulties, neurological abnormalities
2. Behaves extremely irritably
3. Moves extremely lethargically
4. Exhibits sensory disorientation (can't locate origin of sound and smell)
5. Unresponsive to name being called and/or to noises
6. Screams/cries without tears (many times for no known reason)
7. Exhibits gross-motor delays (walking, running, holding, catching, not potty trained)
8. Exhibits fine-motor delays (pointing, writing, holding utensils, coloring, cutting)
9. Seems to be clumsy (falls a lot, gets hurt, runs into things)

Behavior

1. Displays ultrasensitivity to stimulation (displays primitive behaviors; bizarre reactions to normal noise, pain, touch, smell)
2. Carries out self abuse (hits, bites, pinches self)
3. Does not handle changes in established routines appropriately
4. Practices self stimulation (a repetitive touching of any body part, flaps or flips hands, twists hair, etc.)
5. Behaves ritualistically (washes hands repeatedly, lines up crayons in a box, etc.)
6. Dislikes being touched, affectionately or aversively
7. Demonstrates poor transitional skills (moving from one activity to the next)
8. Behavior worsens with unstructured environment
9. Demonstrates no consistency in appropriate behaviors
10. Shows a dislike/hostility toward nearly everyone
11. Acts aggressively (fights at the drop of a hat...kicks, pinches, bites, pushes)
12. Has spontaneous, uncontrollable temper tantrums and/or hysteria (laughter)
13. Exhibits oppositional behavior (resistant to some/most adult directions)
14. Seemingly lacks fear
15. Shows no remorse for wrongdoing (denies everything)
16. Displays hyperactivity (impulsivity)

Intellectual

1. Exhibits impaired play skills (throws a car, pushes a ball)
2. Does not seem to understand object functionality (does not know what to do with a pencil)
3. Has attention deficits (restless; short attention, distractible, poor concentration)
4. Behaves perseveratively (repeats same action or statement, e.g., colors entire desk)
5. Shows a preoccupation with objects (stares, twirls, sways)
6. Has poor understanding of spatial orientation (on, up, under, etc.)
7. Experiences academic problems (functioning one or more years below chronological age-peers in most subjects)
8. Exhibits phobias (unusual fears, e.g., fear of stuffed toys)
9. Unable to sequence (simple picture story, activities)
10. Experiences processing delays (difficulty solving and answering simple problems)
11. Poor task organization (disorganized, seems unable to get all materials needed to do an activity, does not seem to know what to do first or next, etc.)
12. Speaks with language delays (poor vocabulary understanding)

B. Completed Sample of PDD CHARACTERISTICS Checklist

On page 108, you will find the **Pervasively Developmentally Delayed Characteristics Checklist** to reproduce for use with your students. The completed sample on the following page will show you how to use the form.

NOTE: An alternate version of this checklist is provided on the end of the **Developmental Ages Checklist** (page 112) for those who prefer using less paper.

PERVASIVELY DEVELOPMENTALLY DELAYED CHARACTERISTICS CHECKLIST

NAME Eugene   DOB 1-12-86   DATE 11-6-91   TEACHER Kirkland

CHECK ALL THAT APPLY:

COMMUNICATION
- [x] 1. inappropriately expresses needs
- [ ] 2. little eye contact
- [ ] 3. makes unusual sounds
- [ ] 4. smiles rarely; almost never laughs
- [x] 5. flat affect
- [x] 6. trouble relating to people
- [x] 7. unintelligible (articulation errors)
- [ ] 8. limited verbal responses
- [ ] 9. echolalic
- [ ] 10. abnormal speaking voice
- [ ] 11. off topic responses

PHYSICAL/MOTOR SKILLS
- [ ] 1. multiple health problems _asthma_ _vision problems_
- [x] 2. extremely irritable
- [ ] 3. extremely lethargic
- [x] 4. sensory disorientation
- [ ] 5. unresponsive
- [x] 6. screams/cries without tears
- [x] 7. gross motor delays
- [x] 8. fine motor delays
- [x] 9. seems to be clumsy

BEHAVIOR
- [ ] 1. ultrasensitive to stimulation
- [ ] 2. self abusive
- [ ] 3. doesn't handle routine changes
- [ ] 4. self stimulation
- [ ] 5. has ritualistic behaviors
- [ ] 6. dislikes being touched
- [x] 7. poor transitioning skills
- [x] 8. behavior worsens in unstructured environment
- [x] 9. no consistency in behavior
- [x] 10. shows dislike/hostility to most
- [ ] 11. aggressive
- [x] 12. temper tantrums and/or hysteria
- [x] 13. oppositional behavior
- [x] 14. seeming lack of fear
- [x] 15. shows no remorse
- [x] 16. hyperactive/impulsive

INTELLECTUAL
- [ ] 1. impaired play skills
- [ ] 2. poor object functionality
- [x] 3. attention deficits
- [ ] 4. perseverative
- [ ] 5. shows a preoccupation with objects
- [x] 6. poor spatial orientation
- [x] 7. academic problems
- [ ] 8. phobias
- [x] 9. unable to sequence
- [x] 10. processing delays
- [x] 11. poor task organization
- [x] 12. language delays

Notes/Recommendations Eugene is living in his third foster home since Christmas, 1990. He has been there for only two weeks. The foster parents say Eugene is not adjusting easily to their home. He is destructive and shows no remorse for wrong-doing.

Very active in classroom. Appears unable to attend to any task - even play - for more than 2 minutes. (Check with school nurse on Monday about getting physical to determine if Eugene is hyperactive or ADD.)

Speech is halting and he often stops speaking and stares off into space.

Odont-Winn/Dunagan, 1991

C. Explanation and Instructions for Completing the COMMUNICATION/BEHAVIOR PROMPTS Form

If possible, take time to watch how your suspected PDD child interacts with the other children during structured and free time. If you cannot observe without too many distractions, then ask your school counselor, speech/language specialist, or any other professional, to help you analyze what the child really is doing in your classroom.

During one-on-one interaction, try some of these activities to encourage an immediate response from a child who seems to be "from another planet." Make sure you have gone over this information at least once, so there will be an easy transition from one item to the next. Use this information when completing the **Communication/Behavior Prompts Form** at the back of the book.

1. When you say, "(child's name) come," does the child come on command? (Children who do are functioning at least at a two-year-old level.)

2. Put an object in a paper bag/box/purse. Look in it. Close the bag and shake it. Hold it out away from the child. What does the child do? (Children who reach for the bag without speech are at one year; if they use speech, they are at two plus.)

3. Put some food (snack/fruit) in a baby food jar. Screw the lid down tightly. Put the jar in front of the child. You can also do the same thing with a bottle of bubbles. (Children who cry and make no attempt to open the jar are below one year. If they reach out and attempt to unscrew the lid, two years; if they ask for help, two years plus.)

4. Roll a toy car to the child and observe response. (Children who roll the car back are at two plus.)

5. Exchange the car for a ball. Hand the ball to the child. (Children who change easily from one activity to another are at two to three years.)

6. Wind up a toy. Let it "run down" on the table in front of the child. Hand the toy to the child. (Children who scream are at one year. If they reach out for help, one year plus; if they use words, two years; if they use a phrase, three years.)

7. Give the child a simple picture on a sheet of paper with verbal instructions to color it, but do not indicate a color. Hold the crayons in your hand. (Children who ask/sign/reach for crayons, two years of age; any less is below two.)

8. Give the child a blank piece of paper. Ask the child to draw a picture of himself or herself. (Four years if the drawing has a head, body, eyes; five years if a face and extremities are included.)

9. Use two toy phones. Pick yours up and say "Hello." What does the child do with the phone? (Children who say "Hi," or "Hello," are at two years of age; if there is conversation, three to four years of age.)

10. Hold up two puppets. Ask, "Which one do you want?" If the child does not choose, give him/her one. With your puppet say, "Hi." What does the child do? (If the child talks using the puppet, three to four years.)

11. Sit with the child and have him or her turn the pages in a book while you read the words. As you read, what does the child do? (Children who turn two to three pages at a time are at two years of age. If they turn pages singly, three years. If they use one to two words, two years of age; three or more words, at least three years of age.)

12. Give the child a ten-piece (maximum) puzzle to put together. (Four-year-olds can put together a simple 5–7-piece puzzle. At five, they can put together an 8–10-piece puzzle.)

13. Ask "Where's your _____?" Name ten body parts, one at a time. Can the child touch eyes, hands, nose, feet, hair, ears, mouth, arms, legs, tummy? (Children who can touch all ten body parts are at three years.)

14. Give the child five blocks to stack. If successful, give the child one block at a time up to ten. (Children who stack five are at two years; eight to ten blocks, three years.)

15. Give the child a brush, comb, washcloth, toothbrush, and a doll. What does the child do with each item? Another approach would be to give a plate, spoon, cup, bowl, doll. (Children who use the objects according to true function are at two to three years.)

16. Give the child a set of rings and a pole and instruct him or her to stack the rings on the pole from largest to smallest. (Children who stack them correctly are at three years.)

Materials to Use in Completing the COMMUNICATIONS/BEHAVIOR PROMPTS Form

bag/box/purse (things that close)
baby food jar
food (raisins, dry cereal, etc.)
jar of bubbles
rolling object (car, truck, etc.)
ball
wind-up toy
paper with simple picture
blank paper
crayons
two toy telephones
two puppets
books (up to five)
puzzles (simple and complex—up to ten pieces)
ten blocks
brush, comb
toothbrush
washcloth
doll
plate, bowl
cup, spoon
stacking rings and a pole

D. Completed Sample of the COMMUNICATION/BEHAVIOR PROMPTS Form

At the back of the book, you will find the **COMMUNICATION/BEHAVIOR PROMPTS Form** to reproduce for use with your students. The completed sample on the following page will show you how to use the form.

Communication/Behavior Prompts

Name: Eugene   Date: 11-7-91   Evaluator: Kirkland

1. Say, "__Eugene__ come." What does the child do?
   He came after 3 requests.

2. Put an object in a paper bag/box/purse. Look in it. Close it and shake it. Hold it out away from the child. What does the child do?
   Snatched bag from me, threw it down and stamped on it.

3. Put some food (snack/fruit) in a baby food jar, or blow some bubbles and put the wand back into the jar. Screw the lid down tightly. Put the jar in front of the child. What does the child do? * NO SPEECH
   Attempted to unscrew lid. Beat jar on table. Handed to me.

4. Roll a toy car to the child. What does the child do?
   Pushed it back to me (hard). Said "Vroom, vroom"

5. Exchange the car for a ball. Hand the ball to the child. What does the child do?
   Threw ball away (behind him). Used left hand.

6. Wind up a toy. Let it "run down" on the table in front of the child. Hand the toy to the child if he/she doesn't take it. What does the child do?
   Attempted to wind. One turn only. Pushed car away/averted head.

7. Give the child a simple picture on a sheet of paper. Tell the child to color it, but DO NOT give a crayon. Hold the colors in your hand. What does the child do?
   Eugene took all the crayons. Scribbled on sheet (not in lines).

8. Give the child a piece of paper and crayons and say, "Draw a picture of you." What does the child do?
   He drew a BIG head, little body with no extremities. Eyes, mouth. *No Nose.

9. Hand the child a toy phone. Pick up your phone and say "HELLO." What does the child do?
   Said "Hello."

10. Hold up two puppets. Ask, "Which one do you want?" If the child does not show a preference, just give the child one. Then say, "HELLO." What does the child do?
    Said "Hello" and put puppet towards me. Immediately gave puppet back.

11. Begin reading and turning the pages in a book. What does the child do?
    Grabbed book. Turned several pages at once. Tore one out.

12. Give the child an 8-to-10 piece puzzle. What does the child do?
    Attempted. Reached for my hand to help him.

13. Ask, "Where's your _____" (eyes, hands, nose, feet, hair, ears, mouth, arms, legs, tummy). What does the child do?
    Knew eyes, nose, ears, mouth, hair.

14. Give the child five blocks to stack. If successful, give additional blocks one at a time up to ten. What does the child do?
    Built a 7-block tower. When eighth tottered, knocked tower down.

15. Give the child a brush, comb, washcloth, toothbrush and a doll OR give a plate, spoon, cup, bowl, and a doll. What does the child do?
    Fed doll, stirred in bowl. Said "Eat!"

16. Give a set of rings and a pole. Say, "Stack them from largest to smallest." What does the child do?
    Refused to attempt.

Odom-Winn/Dunagan, 1991

E. Explanation and Instructions for Completing the DEVELOPMENTAL AGES CHECKLIST

The following stages are merely a general guide to help you understand how old the child is developmentally. Just as the PDD characteristics bleed into different categories, the behaviors described below may appear at slightly different ages depending on whose chart you are reading. There are many developmental charts on the market, and we have made a list of our own. It really does not matter which chart you use as long as you understand how to use it to your benefit in teaching that special child in your classroom. This will help you keep your expectations and frustrations to a minimum. (For example, five-year-olds who are at a two-year-old level developmentally in some areas cannot be expected to perform in those areas at the same level as their peers.)

Use these explanations to help you fill out the **Developmental Ages Checklist** found at the back of the book. You will find a completed sample on pages 17 and 18.

Five-year-olds who are at a two-year-old level developmentally in some areas cannot be expected to perform in those areas at the same level as their peers.

By One Year

1. Uses some gestures and sounds to communicate wants
2. Consistently uses consonant vowel combinations for babbling/pre-speech
3. Uses some words consistently (could use the same word to label everything)
4. Attempts to imitate oral sounds
5. Responds to own name
6. Vocalizes to his or her image in a mirror
7. Makes eye contact
8. Quiets down when picked up
9. Welcomes hugging and touching
10. Responds to people differently
11. Responds to facial expression
12. Laughs at social play
13. Smiles/giggles
14. Entertains self for five minutes
15. Drinks from a cup with assistance
16. Picks up spoon by the handle
17. Holds bottle
18. Feeds self small pieces of food
19. Waits patiently for others to do something for him or her

By Two Years

1. Uses multiple gestures and sounds to communicate intent
2. Consistently articulates *h, p, b, m, n*
3. At eighteen months, has twenty-word vocabulary
4. By twenty-four months, has 200 to 500-word vocabulary
5. Uses words in combinations for simple phrases (two to three words)
6. Uses single words to direct caregivers' attention to specific objects
7. Attempts several strategies for communication if the first is not understood
8. Attends to one activity for at least three minutes
9. Refers to self by name
10. Claims objects as "mine"
11. Hands over object to outstretched hand when told, "Give me..."
12. Responds to praise from adults
13. Hugs, shows affection
14. Plays by self for ten minutes
15. Rolls ball/car back and forth to another person
16. Indicates wet/soiled pants
17. Drinks from a cup independently
18. Feeds self with a spoon
19. Shares some toys (offers toy to another child)
20. Goes to a specified location (chair, bathroom)
21. Follows up to two simple directions (stand up/clap your hands)
22. Matches objects based on color
23. Groups objects by kind
24. Identifies at least five body parts
25. Names/points to pictures (in group) when asked, "What's that?"
26. Turns pages in book two or three at a time
27. Builds a tower of eight blocks
28. Imitates gross- and fine-motor acts reliably
29. Uses objects correctly for functionality (cup/drink; brush/comb hair)

By Three Years

1. Consistently articulates *t, w, k, g, f, ng, y, d*
2. Has a vocabulary of 700-800 words
3. Uses longer word combinations (three to four words)
4. Uses pronouns (*you, me, we*) and some adjectives
5. Asks for objects not in the immediate environment
6. Takes turns during conversations
7. Toileting completed (has infrequent accidents)
8. Stacks five rings in order from largest to smallest on a pole
9. Walks up and down stairs alternating feet

10. Complies with simple requests 50% of the time
11. Talks for a doll/puppet
12. Uses refusal to control
13. Plays next to, but only occasionally with, other children
14. Attends to one group activity for five to ten minutes
15. Engages in simple make-believe
16. Verbally indicates toileting needs
17. Follows simple rules
18. Stacks tower of at least nine blocks
19. Strings large beads
20. Folds square paper with a crease
21. Turns pages in a book singly
22. Performs motions to songs
23. Draws a circle and horizontal line from a model
24. Cooperates by paying attention when being taught a new skill
25. Interacts positively with peers
26. Laughs at silly behavior
27. Follows a sequence of three instructions (three steps)
28. Names primary colors (when asked, "What color is this?")
29. Points out correct size (when asked *big/little; tall/short*)
30. Twists (turns) door knobs/lids
31. Uses same objects for several purposes (cubes: tower, table, cars, train, etc.)

By Four Years

1. Consistently articulates *r, s, sh, ch, th, l, v*
2. Speaks in complete sentences (four to eight words in length)
3. Has a vocabulary in excess of 1,500 words
4. Places endings on words
5. Uses noun-verb agreement, contractions, and past tense
6. Uses articles (*the, a, an*) and prepositions (*on, in, under*) in sentences
7. Begins to use words with abstract meaning (*sad, afraid*)
8. Imitates three or four-word phrases correctly
9. Follows simple rules and procedures in the classroom
10. Attends to a self-directed activity for fifteen minutes
11. Attends to group activity ten to fifteen minutes with little prompting
12. Attempts task alone before verbally asking for help
13. Recites memorized verbal sequences from day to day (alphabet, numbers one to twenty, poems)
14. Initiates peer contact/play
15. Says "please" and "thank you" spontaneously
16. Expresses positive emotions
17. Talks briefly on the telephone
18. Shows sympathy
19. Uses imagination in playing to create characters and materials

20. Tells a story with no theme or plot
21. Carefully uses items that belong to others
22. Distinguishes between fact/fantasy
23. Plays contentedly in a small group
24. Shows fondness by offering hugs, kisses, and help
25. Buttons/unbuttons large buttons
26. Catches bouncing ball
27. Stands on one foot two to three seconds
28. Matches circle, triangle, square
29. Strings small beads
30. Draws people with head, body, eyes

By Five Years

1. Consistently articulates the *s, r,* and *l* blends
2. Has a vocabulary which exceeds 2,000 words
3. Uses adverbs, future tense, and present tense
4. Uses all pronouns, personal pronouns, and articles correctly
5. Uses sentences that are eight words or longer
6. Attends to group games involving orderly turn taking
7. Has a favorite friend
8. Reads numbers one to ten, then later ten to twenty
9. Answers telephone correctly
10. Listens to a set of classroom directions
11. Behaves appropriately in different situations (library, lunchroom, music)
12. Expresses own feelings in words
13. Expresses how others feel
14. Asks for help instead of getting angry or going on to another activity
15. Skips on alternating feet
16. Kicks large moving ball
17. Bounces and catches ball in hands (not against the body)
18. Cuts along lines with scissors
19. Prints numbers and letters from a model
20. Puts together eight- to ten-piece puzzle
21. Draws people with face, body, extremities
22. Tells a story with a simple plot
23. Groups objects in a variety of categories
24. Sequences objects by degree (size: small to large; color: light to dark, etc.)
25. Completes "what comes next" drawings
26. Understands how objects are alike and different
27. Makes possible suggestions for solving a problem
28. Persists at tasks in spite of distractions (sounds, people)
29. Rearranges objects to match original sequence

DEVELOPMENTAL AGES CHECKLIST

NAME _Eugene_ DOB _1-12-86_ DATE _11-6-91_ TEACHER _Kirkland_

INSTRUCTIONS: CHECK EACH BEHAVIOR THAT YOU FEEL THE CHILD EXHIBITS MORE THAN 50% OF THE TIME.

BY ONE YEAR
1. Uses some gestures and sounds
2. Uses consonant vowel combinations
3. Uses some words
4. Attempts to imitate oral sounds
5. Responds to own name
6. Vocalizes in a mirror
7. Makes eye contact
8. Quiets down when picked up
9. Welcomes touching
10. Responds to people differently
11. Responds to facial expression
12. Laughs at social play
13. Smiles/giggles
14. Entertains self for 5 minutes
15. Drinks from a cup with assistance
16. Picks up spoon by the handle
17. Holds bottle
18. Feeds self
19. Waits patiently

all achieved

BY TWO YEARS
1. ✓ Uses multiple gestures and sounds
2. ✓ Articulates h, p, b, m, n
3. ___ 20 words - 18 months
4. ___ 200-500 words - 24 months
5. ✓ Uses words in combinations
6. ✓ Uses words to direct attention
7. ✓ Attempts to make self understood
8. ___ Attends for 3 minutes
9. ___ Refers to self by name
10. ___ Claims objects as "mine"
11. ✓ Responds to "give me"
12. ✓ Responds to praise
13. ✓ Hugs, shows affection
14. ✓ Plays by self for 10 minutes
15. ✓ Rolls objects back and forth to another
16. ✓ Indicates wet/soiled pants
17. ✓ Drinks from cup
18. ✓ Eats with a spoon
19. ✓ Shares some
20. ___ Goes to specified location
21. ___ Follows two simple directions
22. ___ Matches based on color
23. ___ Groups objects by kind
24. ✓ Identifies five body parts
25. ✓ Names/points to pictures
26. ✓ Turns two or three pages at a time
27. ___ Builds eight block tower
28. ___ Imitates gross/fine motor acts
29. ✓ Uses objects correctly

BY THREE YEARS
1. ___ Articulates t, w, k, g, f, ng, y, d
2. ___ Vocabulary of 700-800 words
3. ___ 3-4 word combinations
4. ___ Uses some pronouns and adjectives
5. ___ Asks for distant objects
6. ___ Turn-takes in conversation
7. ✓ Toileting completed
8. ___ Stacks five rings in order
9. ✓ Walks up and down stairs alternating feet
10. ✓ Complies with simple requests
11. ___ Talks for a doll/puppet _Only "HELLO"_
12. ✓ Uses refusal to control
13. ✓ Plays next to other children
14. ___ Attends with group 5-10 minutes
15. ___ Engages in simple make-believe
16. ✓ Verbally indicates toileting needs
17. ___ Follows simple rules
18. ___ Stacks 9 block tower
19. ✓ Strings large beads
20. ___ Folds paper with crease
21. ___ Turns pages singly
22. ___ Performs motions to songs
23. ___ Draws from a model
24. ___ Pays attention when being taught
25. ___ Interacts positively with peers
26. ___ Laughs at silly behavior
27. ___ Follows three step instructions
28. ___ Names primary colors
29. ___ Points out correct size
30. ___ Turns door knobs/lids
31. ___ Uses same objects for several purposes

More than 50% (15/29) checked in 2-year category. Only had 7/31 in 3-year. Only two in 4-year and one in 5-year.

CLASSIFY as 2½-year old, with emerging 3-year old characteristics.

Odom-Winn/Dunagan

DEVELOPMENTAL AGES CHECKLIST (con't)

BY FOUR YEARS

___ 1. Articulates r, s, sh, ch, th, l, v
___ 2. Speaks in complete sentences
___ 3. 1500 word vocabulary
___ 4. Places endings on words
___ 5. Uses correct grammar
___ 6. Uses articles and prepositions
___ 7. Uses abstract words
✓ 8. Imitates 3-4 word phrases
___ 9. Follows rules
___ 10. Self-directed for 15 minutes
___ 11. Attends with group 10 to 15 minutes
___ 12. Attempts task before asking for help
___ 13. Recites memorized sequences
___ 14. Initiates peer contact/play
___ 15. Says "please" and "thank you"
___ 16. Expresses positive emotions
___ 17. Talks briefly on the telephone
___ 18. Shows sympathy
___ 19. Uses imagination in play
___ 20. Tells a plotless story
___ 21. Carefully uses other's items
___ 22. Distinguishes between fact/fantasy
___ 23. Plays contentedly in a small group
___ 24. Shows fondness
✓ 25. Buttons/unbuttons large buttons
___ 26. Catches bouncing ball
___ 27. Stands on foot 2-3 seconds
___ 28. Matches circle, triangle, square
___ 29. Strings small beads
___ 30. Draws people with head, body, eyes

BY FIVE YEARS

___ 1. Articulates s, r, l blends
___ 2. 2000 word vocabulary
___ 3. Uses adverbs and tenses
___ 4. Uses all pronouns and articles
___ 5. Uses eight word sentences
___ 6. Plays turn-taking group games
___ 7. Has a favorite friend
___ 8. Reads numbers to 20 correctly
___ 9. Answers telephone correctly
___ 10. Listens to directions
___ 11. Behaves in different situations
___ 12. Expresses own feelings
___ 13. Expresses how others feel
___ 14. Asks for help
___ 15. Skips on alternating feet
___ 16. Kicks large moving ball
___ 17. Bounces and catches ball in hands
___ 18. Cuts along lines with scissors
___ 19. Prints numbers and letters
___ 20. Puts together 8-10 piece puzzle
✓ 21. Draws people with face, body, extremities ? *(NO NOSE)*
___ 22. Tells story with a simple plot
___ 23. Groups by category
___ 24. Sequences by degree
___ 25. Completes "what comes next" drawings
___ 26. Understands alike and different
___ 27. Makes suggestions
___ 28. Persists at tasks
___ 29. Rearranges objects in original sequence

Notes *Appeared uninterested in any task requiring fine motor skills. Had to be physically held in story circle. Toileting complete. Follows only very simple instructions. K.*

F. Ready, Set, Begin!

You have now completed the following three informational forms:
* **Pervasively Developmentally Delayed Characteristics Checklist**
* **Communication/Behavior Prompts Form**
* **Developmental Ages Checklist**

You may be thinking, "What in the world do we do now that we have tested, evaluated, measured, and checklisted this PDD child?" First, let's take a look at what you now know about this particular child.

You know:

1. The child's approximate developmental age
2. The characteristics that make the child different in four areas: communication, physical/motor skills, behavior, and intellect
3. How the child compares with his or her classmates
4. What the child can and cannot do (will, will not?)
5. Where you need to begin in order to teach this child.

You now have a word picture, statistics for comparison, deficits, and skills of a PDD child. How do you translate this factual information into a realistic, usable plan of action?

We believe that any education involves taking children from where they are currently functioning, regardless of where that is, to a higher level. It sounds so simple, and it is, once you have determined where each child is and where you want him or her to go. In the following pages we will give you a sort of "road map" to guide you in your quest to educate PDD children. Before you begin, you must remember that each child's route is different, and there are unexplained detours, major road blocks, and unexpected twists. These, along with stormy weather, could prevent arrival at the destination on time. That doesn't mean that the child won't get there, but there will be delays.

View the child as a whole being. Anything less is unfair to the child. All areas of development are a part of the child's education. Unless you know where the child has been, you cannot fairly determine where he or she is going. The checklists, forms, and explanations have been formulated to give you all the necessary data to initiate a comprehensive educational plan for crack kids and other pervasively developmentally delayed children.

View the child as a whole being. Anything less is unfair to the child. All areas of development are a part of the child's education.

Physical prompts are essential...without guided practice, nothing will happen.

Here's a simple plan of action for you to use to devise a program of instruction:

1. Look at the two completed short forms (**Developmental Ages Checklist** and the **PDD Characteristics Checklist**) simultaneously.

   A. Decide the approximate developmental age of the child.
   B. Target deficit areas on the Developmental Ages Checklist that you want to begin improving immediately. (We use a brightly colored pen to circle the numbers on the checklist). You will NOT want to begin with those behaviors that you have checked as performed more than 50% of the time.
   C. Look at the checked characteristics on the PDD Form. Choose one to three items from each of the four areas. These are the characteristics that you want to modify first.
   D. Determine which other professionals, e.g. physical therapists, may be involved with the education of this particular child. If possible, enlist the assistance of one of these experts in setting up goals and implementing your educational plan for the child.

2. Using the lesson plan form you are most comfortable with, write down (in simple language) the skills you want the child to acquire within the framework of your regular lesson plans. Crack kids and other PDD children will be able to participate in some of the regular activities of the day. It is imperative that they be included as much as possible.

Social development is a critical issue with PDD children. Just because they appear to be totally oblivious to your "normal" routine does not mean that they are not picking up information subliminally. For example, suppose you want the PDD children in your class to acquire coloring skills. When the entire class begins a coloring project, give the same activity sheet to the crack kids, even if they cannot hold a jumbo crayon. Help each PDD child develop the coloring action by guiding his or her hand. Praise any attempt by the child to color alone.

See how easy that was? Only two simple steps are needed to prepare your plan of instruction. The rest of this book is designed to assist you in every facet of instruction, not only for the crack kid, but also for any PDD child. Look at these children as possible space travelers...not as "space cadets."

Room Set-Up   2

A. What to Do When...

The tips below are simply suggestions to help you get your room organized in the most efficient manner to deal with one or more crack kids. These ideas will also work in a regular classroom with "regular" children.

1. ALWAYS position yourself as near the door as possible. PDD children are notorious runners, and you'll need very quick arms to keep them in the room if they don't wish to stay and play with you.

2. If you sit down, don't have anything restricting your ability to get up and out of your desk chair in a flash. Many times if you can grab the child immediately, he or she will more easily accept staying in the room.

3. If you have to use tables, place them as far apart as possible. Consider having your play area in the center of the room, with learning centers around the perimeter of the class walls.

4. Using individual desks is a big advantage with PDD children. The desks can be changed to suit your needs once the child understands that the desk with the blue triangle is his or hers no matter where it is located. Keeping the children separated from one another as much as possible is a good strategy, too. Most young children do not yet possess the social graces, so keeping them apart is a good plan.

5. If you have a large room with ample equipment, there are many possible arrangements. We have our preschool room divided into quadrants. The children learn very early that they transition from one area to another. The play area is cordoned off with shelves. The shelves face into the play area and hold the items with which they may play during their time on the play rug.

6. If your classroom is small, use a whole-room seating plan. In other words, put the chairs/tables/desks all over the room. You can then fill in with your learning centers, play areas, and *quiet chair*.

7. Every classroom with a PDD child should also be equipped with a quiet chair. Of course, the chair is not quiet, but, hopefully, the occupant will become that way once he or she is seated in it. We find that the quiet chair works very well with PDD children once they understand that until their bottom touches the seat (facing

Every classroom with a PDD child should also be equipped with a quiet chair.

When a child leaves the quiet chair, offer praise for getting control.

in the proper direction, of course) and their little mouths are shut and no sounds are forthcoming they must remain there. The quiet chair can be very important in teaching your other children that they, too, must follow directions. The quiet chair needs to be set apart, almost hidden if possible. We have them behind study carrels, beside file cabinets, in a corner, etc. The beauty of this little chair is that it is not aversive. The child makes the decision when to leave the chair, although we make our younger ones wait until they are told to leave. Our older children know that once we put them in the chair, all they have to do is get quiet and still. When they have done so, they are allowed to get up and rejoin their classmates. When a child leaves the quiet chair, offer praise for getting control. This includes hugs and verbal reinforcement: "I knew you would do it; I'm very happy that you get to come and join the group." PDD children, as a general rule, do not understand the abstract concept of the consequences of behavior, but they do understand the importance of not getting put in the nasty quiet chair.

8. Look at your room carefully. Where is the best place to put the computer? The games? The toys? The aquarium? The quiet chair? The water table? Do you have a rocking chair at home? Will it fit here? How about a green plant and a colorful wall hanging? These are great items to add to your reading center or corner. Our responsibility to educate does not stop with the placement of chairs, the provision of nourishing food, the teaching of alphabet and numbers, and the supervision of play. We are also responsible for making the children feel comfortable and safe within the walls of the classroom. The ambience in your classroom is as important to all of your students as the ambience of your living room is to you.

Many PPD children have never been to a school and will have absolutely no idea what those desks could possibly have to do with them.

9. If you know that you will have one or more crack kids in your classroom, please put some thought into where those children will be placed. They are already different and will not adapt very quietly and calmly to this latest change in their environment. Many of them have never been to a school and will have absolutely no idea what those desks could possibly have to do with them. Most likely, the PDD children will simply react to the change much like a cat does when you cage it to go to the veterinarian. The child's caretaker can probably tell you if the child will sit without assistance.

10. If one of your PDD children happens to be the strong, silent type, pay special attention to where that child sits. He or she will require constant and consistent stimulation to get any response. Other PDD children need calm, serene surroundings in which to function, which may sound impossible. It isn't, but it is pretty difficult.

You may have to make some adjustments after the first few days. This will require a delicate touch on your part. After all, you did tell Tommy that his desk would always be the one in the second row with the red circle on it, and he has that matching red ball clutched in his hand every single morning. You *can* make seating changes though! In fact, it may be the only thing you can do to salvage that first week. Although we feel consistency is critical, we also know that anything written in stone will require some refining and polishing. Once you realize that you have made a seating or arrangement error, don't hesitate to change it. Rigidity will not hold you in good stead while working with any child, but especially not with the PDD child.

11. Use storage cubes and baskets as much as possible. It is much easier to train PDD children to pick up a basketful of toys as opposed to an entire play area. Set limits and amounts the first day with toys, blocks, cars, etc. Don't let the children take out too many things, or you will spend the entire afternoon trying to get them to put everything away. NEVER PUT THE ITEMS AWAY YOURSELF. From the very first second, make the children put what they get out back where they got it. With PDD children, you will probably have to put your hands over theirs and move each item back to its place. Trust us, it will be worth the effort in the long run. One day a five-year-old saw a teacher putting away toys that had not been used. He ran over and "signed" to her: "The blocks don't go there. They go here!" This example reassures us that repetitive instructions and consistent carry-through work!

B. Materials: The Dream and the Reality

Every school has some equipment specifically designed for young children in the primary grades. If you played school growing up you know what the basic necessities of life in a classroom are...crayons, paper, pencils, manipulatives, books, toys, and a multitude of assorted odds and ends. Since most of you are already teachers with a room of your own, we have chosen to give you some suggestions and the names of some of the suppliers we use in our systems. This information is neither extensive nor comprehensive. It is simply a base upon which to build your materials inventory.

Although we feel consistency is critical, we also know that anything written in stone will require some refining and polishing. Once you realize that you have made a seating or arrangement error, don't hesitate to change it.

MANIPULATIVES

Manipulatives are small objects that can be used to teach any concept. Remember that math is not the only discipline where manipulatives are incorporated into the curriculum. They are NOT just for counting. Anything you can touch, feel, or move can be a manipulative... toys, utensils, fruit, rocks, clay!

In science, use them for weights. In social studies, manipulatives can be used to teach a unit on transportation. Let the students work with toy cars, trucks, trains, airplanes, boats, and motorcycles. Utilize "trash" manipulatives for three dimensional posters, creature creations, and decorating ceramic/clay bowls.

Any good school supply company can offer you educational manipulatives. Don't limit yourselves to those, however. Go to your local variety store and look for bargains. Arts and crafts stores are also good places to find objects like wiggly eyes, chenille pompoms and stems, beads and a multitude of small wooden shapes. Hardware stores and your kitchen are also good places to "shop."

MANIPULATIVE SUPPLIERS

ABC SCHOOL SUPPLY
POB 100019
DULUTH, GEORGIA 30136
1-800-669-4222

This national supply house has several catalogs that feature both specific need and general materials. They have sales representatives all over the United States. Just call their number, ask for customer service, request a catalog and "voila"...they'll send it to you. We have found the sales representative to be extremely knowledgeable, helpful and willing to present workshops on a variety of topics. We have had workshops on puppets, building blocks, and art given free of charge to several school systems.

THE SCHOOL HOUSE
6601 HAMILTON ROAD
COLUMBUS, GEORGIA 31904
1-404-322-3564

This is our local school supply house. We have found them to be a great asset in assisting less experienced teachers with professional books, bulletin board supplies, general classroom materials, art supplies, and furniture. Most of the employees are, or have been, educators. They will gladly mail you a catalog. If you have a local school supplier, you will most likely find the same courteous help we get at The School House.

LEARNING CENTERS

Learning centers are wonderful inventions for the classroom teacher. They are multipurpose areas where children can run the gamut from fantasy (creating a Loch Ness monster) to using a computer (addition problems).

Learning centers can include listening, arts and crafts, all academic areas, cooking and creativity. Only your imagination can limit you in what kind of learning centers you have in your classroom.

The following is an example of how we have used cooking as a whole language theme and incorporated it into a viable learning center that can be used all year. PDD children are often quite willing to taste anything once. Cooking addresses all five senses, probably better than many other activities.

Cooking Corner

This is a small (or large, if you're fortunate) area set aside in your classroom for kitchen projects. You can start with mixing fruit punch and expand to cooking meals. All you need is a hot plate, running water (or a nearby bathroom), and if feasible a little toaster oven. Food is a powerful teaching tool as well as a terrific reinforcer. One of our teachers has a weekly cooking period in her lesson plans. Students fix at least one item every week. One of their favorites...believe it or not...is low sodium rice cakes with peanut butter, cream cheese and grape jelly.

A simple but fantastically successful menu item is instant pudding "pictures." Put out the instant pudding box. Let one child measure the milk, another pour, another stir. Let one child pass out small pieces of poster board or paper plates. They then use their clean fingers and hands to create a picture. Have you been talking about volcanoes or mountains? Ask them to create one with pudding. Put a smiley face on their completed artwork and let the children eat their assignment. Allow licking of fingers, too. One of our more fastidious PDD children requested the use of a spoon to eat her creation.

Always follow the routine rules of hygiene. Begin and end the activity with clean hands (theirs and yours).

It's nice but not necessary to have child-sized appliances. A cardboard box turned over (even one of your storage bins) can serve as a table or stove. There doesn't need to be a lot of expense involved. *Use your imagination!* Encourage the children to use their own ideas. They can pretend to use a mixer (whirring merrily away at the top of their little lungs) or a can opener clicking, clicking, clicking.

Food is a powerful teaching tool as well as a terrific reinforcer.

Most children today, across all economic levels, have poor imaginations. Television, computer games, video arcades, fantasy movies, and real life have squelched their fanciful, whimsical natures.

Imagination Learning Centers

We have also chosen to extol the virtues of an imagination learning center. Most children today, across all economic levels, have poor imaginations. Television, computer games, video arcades, fantasy movies, and real life have squelched their fanciful, whimsical natures. What a shame! You can help all your children generally, and your PDD kids specifically, by providing them with a safe place to form and create imaginary creatures, people, and places. Remember that many children go home to stark misery. Give them a center to fly away to in your classroom. When we were children, (just prior to Edison inventing the light bulb), the majority of our summer vacations were spent in the back yard, cooking on an imaginary stove drawn in the dirt, and fixing oak leaf hamburgers. Our afternoons were spent making mud pies to be decorated with acorns and served to our daddies when they came home from work. Draw on your own experiences to to help your children find theirs.

How about giving one or more of these a try?

1. Let's Pretend Boxes
Fill old cardboard boxes with grooming supplies, grown-up clothing, cooking utensils, cars/trucks, doll houses, people (cowboys, super heroes, soldiers, miniatures), doctor/nurse kits, tool kits (especially soft or plastic ones). Use real tools if there is adult supervision. Children love to bang hammers on pieces of boards...with or without nails. Garage and yard sales are often bonanzas for filling up a myriad of pretend boxes.

2. Tea Party
If your room is large enough, a play-like eating area is wonderful fun. Have small tables and chairs, tea sets, plates, eating utensils, and glasses. Let the children "pretend" to serve each other meals, cookies, tea, coffee, snacks. Have a box filled with clean, empty veggie cans, gelatin packages, cereal boxes, milk cartons, etc. Ask them to "fix" dinner for you. Let them tell you what they fixed, how they fixed it, and how it tastes. Pretend to eat, and offer praise. Ask how they did it, what they think it might cost to buy it, how big were the boxes the food came in, and if they remember the recipe.

They'll love learning through pretending. If your PDD children are non-verbal, take the time to have them draw pictures of what they have cooked.

3. Box Center
Keep a stack of storage boxes in one area. Label each box and change them regularly. Some suggestions are: transportation (trucks, cars, and other vehicles of various sizes), doll houses (several kinds with/without furniture, people, landscaping items), miniatures

26

(plastic people, animals including super heroes, soldiers and facsimiles of cartoon characters). Let the children make forts, houses, and farms with building/construction blocks, paper and paste.

A child's imagination is one of the most under-used teaching/learning tools available to us. Crack kids inhabit a world all their own most of the time. Their fantasy may be our everyday lives. Their imaginations MUST be cultivated, manipulated and trained. You certainly don't expect to grow prize-winning roses without pruning, shaping, fertilizing, and watering, do you? Through their imagination and the directed activities you provide, all children can come to terms with the world in which they must live.

You can spend almost nothing or mega-bucks on learning centers. If possible, quality computer software should be high on your list of priorities. We have several companies that either deal exclusively in educational software or devote a portion of their production to good, solid programs.

EDUCATIONAL MEDIA SUPPLIERS

CURRICULUM ASSOCIATES
5 ESQUIRE ROAD
N. BILLERICA, MA 01862-2589
1-800-225-0248

Some of their programs include: *The Patient Tutor* series. (One of the neatest things we've seen in a long time comes from this publisher. It is a calendar of home activities for every month of the year. It comes in several grade levels and is a real bonus for parent communication).

EDUCATIONAL ACTIVITIES
PO BOX 392
FREEPORT, NY 11520
1-800-645-3739

Some of their programs include: *Talk To Me, Stop, Look, and Listen* (two voice interaction programs where the child can hear his or her own voice), *ABC–1-2-3 Activities for Learning, Wordfind, Mathematics Worksheet Generator, Adventures of Dobot, The Micro-Gardener, Rov-a-Bot*. Educational Activities also is an excellent supplier of videos. Some of those are: *5 To Get Ready* (a series of readiness skills-activity-music videos), *Learning Basic Skills: Music by Hap Palmer, Listen to Learn, Children's Songs Around the World*, and *Seasons*.

> *A child's imagination is one of the most under-used teaching/learning tools available to us.*

LAUREATE LEARNING SYSTEMS
110 EAST SPRING STREET
WINOOSKI, VERMONT 05404

Some of their programs include: *The Talking Verbs, The Talking Nouns, Words and Concepts I* and *II*, and *Micro-Lads*.

MINNESOTA EDUCATIONAL COMPUTING CORPORATION
3490 LEXINGTON AVENUE N
ST. PAUL, MINN. 55126

Some of their programs include: *The Friendly Computer, Picture Chompers*, and *First Letter Fun*.

SUNBURST COMMUNICATIONS
39 WASHINGTON AVE.
PLEASANTVILLE, NY 10570-9971

Some of their programs include: *Muppet Learning Keys* and *Muppetville*.

BOOKS

Books are the very backbone of education. The more limited the child's communication ability, the more sophisticated the educator's must become. There are thousands of excellent "how-to" books. We have chosen an assortment to list here for ideas. We each have hundreds of books in our own home libraries, ranging from erudite philosophical texts to bulletin board idea books. No one dares trash a book...any book...within two miles of us.

Weekly magazines, newspapers, educational journals, old teacher's editions and many more books provide inspiration for teaching. PDD children push ingenuity to the limit and challenge even the very best educators. If your bookshelves can hold another book, start scavenging. School and public libraries, media centers, archives, doctor's offices, book stores, and the trusty yard sales are a few places to begin your search for fresh ideas. Check with your local school system media centers. Many times when they adopt new textbook series, they discard the old ones.

Do Touch by Labritta Gilbert
The Sun's Not Broken, a Cloud's Just in the Way by Sydney Gurewitz Clemens
Mudpies and Magnets by Robert Williams, Robert Rockwell, and Elizabeth Sherwood
Sourcebook of Language Learning Activities by William Justin Worthley
The Learning Circle by Patty Claycomb
Practical Solutions to Practically Every Problem by Ellen Galinsky

Day In Day Out by Dorothy Michener and Beverly Muschlitz
The Big Book of Practically Everything by Rosemary Alexander
Pocketful of Miracles by Connie Eisenhart
Channels to Children by Carol Beckman, Roberta Simmons, and Nancy Thomas

NOTE: Most of these books were purchased at our local school supply house. There are hundreds of titles and they range from very inexpensive to moderately pricey.

We have decided to list in this section some of the other materials we use in our systems. We are also including some of the screens that we have found useful in determining ability levels and remediation. There are many good screens on the market today. Read up on them, ask to preview for thirty days. Most companies are willing to do this for you.

SCREENING INSTRUMENTS

The Brigance® Inventories—This is a series of assessment books that cover early childhood through high school. They are helpful not only in assessing; but also in giving strategies for remediation and even Individualized Education Plan objectives. Curriculum Associates carries this screen.

Early Language Milestone Scale—The Speech Bin carries this screen.

Battelle Developmental Inventory—DLM carries this screen. We have used it for several years in our preschool programs.

Burks Behavior Rating Scale, Preschool—Western Psychological Services carry this scale. It is an excellent screening tool as well as giving input in the manual for remediation of specific behavioral problems.

AUGMENTATIVE COMMUNICATION SYSTEMS

The Q Solution—This is a unit that uses a laser wand to read bar code symbols. It has black line drawings and a variety of workbooks. The nonverbal PDD child can learn to use the wand and can "read and speak" the words in each workbook. The workbooks have excellent vocabularies and offer the student a way to communicate that is high-tech. This is carried by Curriculum Associates.

The WOLF Communication System—This is a communication board that is portable. We currently have three different programs. The board, while fairly expensive, is versatile and there is almost no limit to the uses in the classroom. We use it with our PDD population at fast food restaurants. It allows the child the independence to place his/her own order by pushing the correct symbol. The WOLF communication board then talks and tells the order taker what the child wants to eat. It is fantastic!

ECHO IIb Speech Synthesizer—This is a piece of equipment that gives your Apple computer an unlimited vocabulary. The voice is human-like and the kids can understand it. The Speech Bin carries this product.

TOUCH WINDOW—This is a portable, touch-sensitive screen that lets you access the computer by simply touching the screen with any blunt pointing tool or your finger. It allows the physically– as well as sensorily–impaired student to use the computer. The Speech Bin also carries this product.

This final note: All the equipment and material in the world does not take the place of one determined, CALM, and caring teacher. Enthusiasm and knowledge educates children, even when they don't want to learn. Money helps, but is not a prerequisite. YOU can create a marvelous learning environment with old clothes, contact paper, beat up pots, and yard sale acquisitions…junk, in other words. Use your imagination, don't be afraid to try new ideas and above all—NEVER GIVE UP!!

Getting Control 3

Do not underestimate the importance of establishing order the first day. Even more so, do not think for a second that getting PDD children to sit in their own seats the first day is not particularly necessary. Trust us, it is!

Before we detail ways to take control of the crack kid, specifically, and your entire class, generally, let's look at a few basics for PDD children who are chronologically between four and six years old.

1. Chances are that communication skills in PDD children will be sadly lacking. They may speak hesitantly or they may utter only guttural, unintelligible sounds. Watch for any indication that they are making an effort to communicate with you. Try to match this communication. If they are speaking in one-word utterances, do the same with them. If they are using only gestures, use gestures and one-word utterances together.

2. Be gentle, but never let your gentleness be mistaken for wimpiness. Firmness with caring is vital to these children. Your first inclination may be to feel very sorry for them. After having them in your classroom for a few days, though, you may have very different feelings. The key is balance. You are their teacher, in the truest sense of the word. Never forget how necessary you are to these crack kids.

3. If you have made use of the checklists provided in this book, you have a pretty good idea of what's going on with the PDD children. They do not perceive the world in the same manner as do your more normal children and will require special handling. Get some input from your special education staff, psychologists for your school, medical personnel, and your administrative team. HAVE A PLAN, if possible, in place as soon as you have determined that you have one or more PDD students in your class. Keep the plan short and sweet. The more convoluted your approach, the less likely you are to meet with success.

Helen Everett, a Georgia educator, writes, "I remind my teachers never to address a behavior unless you are willing to follow through with it, whatever it takes–as long as it takes. Otherwise, ignore it."

4. Find out as much as possible about the PDD children assigned to your class. Ask questions, even if you are told to mind your own business. Determine what agencies are involved, then talk to them. Meet the parents, if possible. If the parents are not involved, insist on meeting the primary caretaker(s). Has the child been to preschool or day care somewhere in the

Never let your gentleness be mistaken for wimpiness.

community? Is the family on public assistance or is it self-sufficient? Are there siblings? Once you have a picture of the child's daily life before public school, you can begin to look for approaches to make his or her in-school behaviors more appropriate. Reading the **Caretaker/Parent Interview Guide Form** at the back of the book, will give you some helpful hints about what kinds of questions to ask.

5. Read up on PDD children. There's not much material published about crack babies, Fetal Alcohol Syndrome, and some of the other lesser-known forms of autism. There is, however, a bountiful supply of articles and books written about autism. Read all you can find. The same characteristics exist to varying degrees in all PDD children. You will find many articles written about the medical aspects of babies exposed prenatally to drugs, especially crack/cocaine. You will find very little written about dealing with these children in school. Even with the enormous amount written about autism, no one seems to have found a real solution or even many successful educational approaches for school-age children. The more you know about the characteristics, the better you will be able to cope with the PDD children in your class.

6. If you are not conversant with the **Individuals with Educational Disabilities Act** or IDEA (PL 94-142) and its amendments, become conversant. This is the U.S. statute covering special education law. Its purpose is to provide disabled students meaningful access to education. There are specific tasks we are mandated to do as public schools to provide a free and appropriate education for these children. Although you may not be directly liable, you are the teacher responsible for the PDD children assigned to your class.

Once you have determined where the PDD children in your classroom are developmentally, you can begin to unlock what is inside. Many crack kids have suffered irreversible brain damage from the mother's or father's use of drugs. (Recent studies indicate that either parent can be responsible for prenatally exposing the fetus to drugs.) This does not mean that the children will never learn, but they will have a much harder time processing, understanding, and retaining information. Some PDD children, predominantly Fetal Alcohol Syndrome and crack babies, have suffered too much brain damage for them to ever experience much success in a regular or even a special educational school setting. These children will eventually be institutionalized, much like the profoundly retarded population. Determining the children's developmental level is crucial.

When you have determined the child's functioning level, read everything you can find on that developmental level. Disregard the chronological age until you are familiar with the developmental level. This will reveal to you where the PDD child fits in your classroom schematic. If a child is six and is functioning like a two-year-old, what do you do? You find out how a two-year-old functions and start there. Do not expect miracles. Do not expect the child to become a six-year-old overnight, developmentally speaking. Do expect slow, small increments of positive change. For example, suppose you have a six-year-old boy in your class who is in his "terrible twos," developmentally. That's exactly how you handle him behaviorally. If he has tantrums, give him natural and logical consequences. Did he disrupt art time with his two-year-old tantrum? Move him away from the fun art time and put him in a quiet chair until he calms down. Then allow him to return. The very instant, however, that he begins to escalate into a tantrum, remove him again. Over and over until he gets the message: No art if you have a tantrum.

Remember that a six-year-old with a two-year-old developmental level feels overwhelmed if you tell him to "Sit down and print your name. Don't get up, don't talk, and act your age!" Teach to the child's developmental age. This is your best bet for changing the child from a negative number to a positive one. It's also your best shot at staying sane.

This chapter deals primarily with getting control within the parameters of your classroom. The information will be simple, to the point, and easy to follow. We will give examples as well as specific guidelines about how to set about getting control of the PDD children in your class.

A. SITTING DOWN

Have you ever thought that if you could only get your PDD children to sit down you would have it made? PDD children don't always like to sit down. Some of them can't sit down (they do not know how). In fact, you will find that many of them simply won't sit down, or worse yet, if you ask them to sit they will stand up immediately!

Let's take a look at some of the intervention strategies you can use when all you want is for the children to sit down in their seats. Experiment with each of them in turn, if that seems best to you, until you find one that works for a particular child. Do not continue to try the first one if the child shows absolutely no signs of sitting. Never assume that the child knows anything. He or she may truly not know how to sit at a desk or in a chair or may not be able to do so without much guidance from you.

If a child is six and is functioning like a two-year-old, what do you do? You find out how a two-year-old functions and start there.

PDD children don't always like to sit down. Many of them simply won't sit down, or worse yet, if you ask them to sit they will stand up immediately!

1. On the first day, have all students line up just inside the door. Personally walk each of the children to their desks, one at a time. As you do, tell them that this is their very own seat. No one may sit in it without the child's (and your) permission. This will work best if you have an aide who can sing with the other children or otherwise occupy their time while they are waiting.

2. Stand in front of the child. Make sure he or she can tell that you mean business by using a firm, but not mean, facial expression. Take the child's hand if he or she will let you and walk together to the assigned seat. Ask or gesture for the child to sit down. Demonstrate, if necessary, by sitting in the child's chair. Get up and "help" the child to sit in it.

3. As you walk with the child, speak softly but firmly, saying, "This is what I want you to do every day when you come into our room." If the child doesn't appear to understand you or doesn't speak in sentences, (1) gesture to the chair and say "Come." Once you get to the seat, (2) gesture again and say "Sit." (See Chapter 4 - Using Our Hands.)

4. If the child gets right back up, repeat steps (1) and/or (2). If he or she spits, curses, runs or cries, repeat your actions all over again and again and again. Consistency will eventually work. It is critical that you establish a routine, keep it simple and do it the same way every time until the child has learned to do it alone.

5. Here's another first day strategy: as children come in the door, have an activity planned that does not require them to be in their seats. You could play musical desks, for example. Play a tape for a few seconds and, when the music stops, whoever you point to goes to his or her own desk. Show the child the desk while the music begins again. Give the seated children a coloring sheet or another "easy" activity to occupy them while the others are being seated.

6. Another strategy to try (if these steps do not work) is the buddy system. At the first sign of trouble, pair every child with a buddy. Child A takes child B to his or her seat and then goes to his or her own chair and sits down. The next day they alternate. Within the first two days, you will know whether your students can/will follow simple one-step directions. If they can help one another and/or follow one another's direction, you will know which children can be your "helpers" in the room.

Still won't sit? Then try any of the following techniques. They are not listed sequentially or in a hierarchy, so just choose the ones that sound feasible for your situation.

1. Give each child a different cutout picture. Have a matching picture taped to the child's seat. Tell the children to find their desks by finding the "twin" picture (We have used simple shapes of different colors as well.) This will let you know right away which students have trouble matching. Remind them to sit down as soon as they find their match. Walk around the room, carefully noting which students find their seats the quickest. Use these students as peer tutors during the first week, and thereafter, if needed.

2. Using the basic plan in (1), substitute a picture of the child taped on the desk. Take the pictures on the first day of class with an instant camera or ask the children's caretakers to send one with them. You will probably be surprised to find out that there are some who do not even recognize their own faces or bodies.

3. If the child simply will not stay in the seat, keep him or her there by:
   (a) sitting next to the child (in a chair) on the "get out" side;
   (b) putting the child's desk next to the wall, and as you give the other students their instructions, keep your knee on the desk frame so that it will not move; or
   (c) asking your paraprofessional/aide or the child's parent/caretaker to keep her or him in the chair for the first few days.

Seating arrangements will probably become very important to you the instant you have a PDD child in your classroom.

Do seating arrangements really matter? Let us suggest that they will probably become very important to you the instant you have a PDD child in your classroom. Preschoolers and kindergartners need to know early on that there are limits set, and PDD children feel this need more profoundly. These limits not only let them know who is in charge, but also allow them to feel safe and secure in this new and possibly frightening environment.

B. Staying Down

Once you get the children to sit down, surely the next step will be easier. Not a chance! After you get them to sit down, you often find that they jump right back up like jack-in-the boxes. What on earth can you do to keep them in their seats?

1. Have something on their desks to "entertain" them—bright pictures, crayons/paper, colored strings, modeling clay, or best of all, food!

2. Use one-word commands until you find out how much the PDD children understand. Couple the one-word utterances with signing (see Chapter 4 for basic signing). If a child appears to be preparing to jump up and run, immediately walk over to him or her and position your body so the child can't get out of the desk.

3. If the child does get away, try one of the strategies from the previous section. Modify and improvise, if necessary. Practice reacting quickly; teachers are supposed to have eyes in back of their heads, you know. Remember that reacting quickly does not mean a jerky movement toward the child. It means thinking about what you are going to need to do and doing it quickly, without threatening gestures.

4. Music soothes the hearts of many PDD children. Have records or tapes handy to put on after the children start getting seated. Whistle (sing) while you work; they may be surprised into being still and trying to figure out how you are making that funny noise!

5. Try putting colored paper shapes of their little hands and feet on the top of their desks and on the floor in front of their seats. Model putting their hands and feet on the taped down shapes. A simple statement, with modeling, of "quiet hands" and "quiet feet" sometimes puts it in perspective for them.

6. For out-of-control children, it may sometimes be necessary to use a restraint harness or a specially manufactured desk such as the *Kinderchair* could be utilized. Commercially-made harnesses are used in many areas on buses for special education children. The harness generally looks like a life preserver with a zipper down the back and loops for the bus seat belt. Harnesses prevent the children from moving around on the bus, hurting others or themselves. Each state, county, city, or school district has made its own decision about restraint. Check with your administrator about local regulations. The safety of the child is paramount.

7. Many PDD children like to thumb through glossy magazines. Encourage that practice once they have learned to come in and sit down with minimum redirection. The magazine will keep them occupied while you get the others ready for their first assignment. Note, however, that many PDD children will look at the same magazine for seven or eight hours, never pausing in their turning of pages. This perseverative behavior keeps them in their own little world, safe from outside influences. If a PDD student uses a magazine in this way, take it away and replace it with a small book that has a few colored pictures (one of the old-fashioned children's reading books).

8. Have a video playing as the students get into their seats. This will distract the more active ones, provide entertainment for those who are suffering from first-week jitters, and give yet others something to pay attention to while you are desperately trying to get everyone in the right seat.

PDD children are much harder to entertain than normal four-, five-, and six-year-olds. Although it is not your responsibility to entertain them, it is your job to establish a routine. Finding innovative ways to keep them in their seats while they are waiting for you to call roll, get lunch count, kiss wounded knees, and the 9,000 other housekeeping chores that keep you busy from daylight 'til dark is your job, too. In Chapter 2, we suggested several publications that will give you some simple quick-to-get-ready projects to occupy waiting time.

C. Looking Up

On-task behavior is not easy to achieve with any young children. It is a Herculean task to help PDD children master it. If you think getting them into the room, sitting down, and staying down have been difficult, just wait!

On-task behavior begins when the child is presented with an assignment. PDD children react in various ways when given a crayon and coloring sheet. Many, however, will simply destroy the sheet and eat the crayons as an afterthought. If the children's developmental age is between two and three years, eating nearly anything, and tearing up paper seems perfectly OK to them. Because they don't know what these items are or what they are used for, these children will not care if you take away the crayons. You must first establish what they like to do and then give them that to do.

For example, suppose your PDD children like raisins. You give them a few raisins, then hand them a crayon and coloring sheet. Put your hand over theirs and show them what you want them to do with the crayon. Show them again and again and again. Say, as you give them the raisins, "If you do what I do, I will give you some more afterwards." For those children who do not speak or only have limited utterances, you could say, "Color picture first." When they do that, immediately give them a raisin, saying "Good." If they allow you to touch them and/or hold their hands in the correct position, say "Great" and give them a raisin. Let go. If they drop the crayon or attempt to eat it, reteach. If they hold it, say "Good" and give them another raisin. Demonstrate again, without using their hands this time, what you want them to do with the crayon. Give them the crayon back. If they even make a move toward putting

PDD children are much harder to entertain than normal four-, five-, and six-year-olds. Although it is not your responsibility to entertain them, it is your job to establish a routine.

crayon to paper, give them another raisin. Does this sound dull and boring? Yes. Does it work? Eventually.

Try some of these other ways to help PDD children stay on-task:

1. PDD children find it very difficult to pay attention for more than a very short period of time. They must have activities planned that take only a minute or so to complete. Some will, however, fasten their eyes on an object and never waver for long periods of time. If your PDD children do this, use it to your advantage. Put an object that they seem visually interested in on their desk. Once they focus on the object, move it to whatever you want them to attend to, such as a paper, book, or television. You may have to do this many times before their eyes will focus on the task you want them to address. Be patient! The children simply do not know what they are supposed to do for you. If you can remember that their behavioral locus of control is all external, you will be able to reach them quicker and have more patience with them.

2. Here is another application of (1). You want the students to put their coats on the coat hooks. With a PDD child who tracks, use an object the child will focus on and move it slowly from directly in front of his or her eyes to the hook. Then, while the child holds the coat, cover the child's hands with yours, move them toward the hook, and place the coat on the hook. Keep the focusing object the same if the child continues to pay attention to it. If that object is no longer interesting, find another one that will attract the child's eyes.

3. Ability to stay on task is essential to the development of communication. Language/vocabulary is very difficult to develop when a child is ultrasensitive to any type of environmental stimulation.

Environmental stimulation includes visual, tactile, auditory, olfactory, and taste. PDD children can be sensitive in one or several areas. Ultrasensitivity to environmental stimuli is exhibited when a child's reaction to stimuli is over-exaggerated.

When you find that a child simply will not attend to, or aggressively resists, any presented task, you will want to determine their area of ultrasensitivity. Once you have ascertained their behavioral rationale, a program of desensitization should be initiated.

Densensitization is a process by which a child is gradually exposed to the very things they fear/dislike. This procedure is done by progressively exposing the child to the feared objects more often and for longer lengths of time. Initially the reactions by the child will be extremely negative. But time and persistence on your part will pay off in the long run.

VISUAL/TACTILE ULTRASENSITIVITY

Let's say that one of your students has a fear of wind-up toys, and refuses to even look at them, much less touch one. Try these steps:

Step 1: Put the unwound toy on a table in front of the child. Either have the child in your lap or beside you. As soon as the child exhibits fear, remove the toy. Repeat until the child can tolerate seeing the toy for one minute. The child should actually be able to touch the toy before moving to Step 2. Note that if the child is so averse to the toy, you may have to let him or her scream while the toy is on the table. Give praise when the child calms down once the toy is removed.

Step 2: Wind the toy in front of the child (don't let the toy touch the child). Hold the toy so that it won't move even though it has been wound a half-turn. Remove the toy as soon as fear is noticed. You may have to physically hold the child NEAR the toy as you are winding it. Repeat until the child is calmer. Remember that this step may take weeks. Don't be discouraged.

Step 3: Allow the toy to move on the table for two to five seconds. Remove the toy. Praise/encourage any ability to remain in control. Continue this until the child can tolerate the toy until it winds down. Once again, this may take many trials.

Step 4: Use Steps 1, 2, and 3 with another toy or two.

Step 5: Have the child hold the toy as you wind it. Only give it a half turn. Increase the time gradually as you wind the toy tighter and tighter. Praise and touch constantly as you are winding the toy and letting the child hold it.

Visual Ultrasensitivity

We saw one child who screamed and fought every time she saw white glue. The parents had already figured out that it was the color and not the texture that she didn't like. Seeing white made her gag. So each day we did one activity geared toward white, such as using white paper for gluing and coloring; we felt, cut, and glued white material; and we even used white finger paints. She expressed her distress loudly and forcefully, but we made her do the activity, if only for a few seconds initially. She can now sit in a chair and will voluntarily look at and touch the white glue without resistance.

Densensitization is done by progressively exposing the child to the feared objects more often and for longer lengths of time.

Tactile Ultrasensitivity

Lots of regular kids don't like to be touched, either. Try continually smiling, speaking softly, and reaching across the table to gently touch their hands, rub their arms, and hug. The touch should only last for a couple of seconds initially, but over a period of time their resistance decreases. They are rigid initially, but gradually they begin to relax and will eventually even reach out their arms to be hugged or touched. Touch is one of the most basic needs a human has, along with food and water. Our children need any positive strokes (verbal, physical) that you can give them. Who knows, you might get a hug on a day you really need one! You must help all the children understand that you, and many of the things in their world, are not going to hurt them. Children should feel secure emotionally before they begin to explore and learn. How do children learn when they continually feel they are in a storm-tossed boat in the middle of a confusing, terrifying, sea? It is your responsibility to give them a "fantasy island" with dry land and an anchor, to help them dock in a safe harbor.

Touch is one of the most basic needs a human has, along with food and water.

Auditory Ultrasensitivity

If you have filled in the **PDD Characteristics Checklist**, use it to determine if the PDD children are ultrasensitive to sounds. If they are, find out the highest level of sound they can tolerate without outward signs of strain. Use that level to get their attention. You may want to utilize headphones so that each child will attend only to the sounds coming through them. Headphones also help him or her attend to the sounds in their own ears. Many PDD children respond to one song with a great deal of attention and passion. (One of our more severely involved students will stop even the most aggressive tantrum when he hears *Are You Sleeping, Brother John?*) Use every external behavior the child exhibits to pair with a behavior you want them to acquire. The "good" behaviors are, in general, internally based.

You might want to come armed with soft ear plugs, a walkman-type cassette player, ear muffs, cotton or a special helmet for ears. The hearing of some PDD children has been found to pick up even the heartbeats of people in their immediate area. This is a substantiated phenomenon. There are several cases where PDD children were finally able to tell about the horrible noises only they could hear, that seemed to bother no one else.

Taste and Smell Ultrasensitivity

Ultrasensitivity to taste and smell can be reduced by consistent exposure to the aversive smell or taste. Reach back in your childhood memories for food or odors you may have found offensive. How did your mother get you to eat rutabagas? Gradually presenting food items usually works. Try disguising the offending taste with a more palatable one. For instance, cover broccoli with melted cheese, or put a piece of melted caramel on a slice of fruit.

Ultrasensitivity, left uncontrolled, will nearly always interfere with teaching on-task behaviors. Some good commercially prepared resources for teaching on-task behaviors are found in Chapter 2. There are also many good books on activities to use with young children to promote and increase on-task behavior. PDD children have a very difficult time, in most instances, remaining on task in the classroom. They need lots of activities of short duration to increase their on-task behavior.

D. Strike Out

PDD children are not always aggressive. They are always different. In this section, we present some methods that can be used to defuse aggressive behaviors in PDD students. These methods have all been tried and proven successful, to some degree, in special education classes. Many of these ideas have also met with at least a modicum of success in regular classes.

Aggressive behavior can be defined as any overt behavior that involves more than one person and could cause physical harm.

In this section we will deal with those aggressive behaviors that involve two or more students. Self-abusive and self-stimulating behaviors will be discussed later.

1. Pulling Hair—This is a favorite of PDD children. When they pull hair, they get a very quick reaction from the owner of the hair! The quickest way to stop hair pulling is to press the aggressor's hand down toward the head of the victim. This action diminishes the pain of the pull, and the surprise of your opposite reaction will give you the needed advantage to remove the child's fingers.

2. Spitting—The best method we have found for dealing with spitters is to make them clean up both the person and the area around where they spat. Cleaning up should be done during a fun activity for the rest of the students whenever possible. Telling crack kids that spitting is nasty will have little or no effect on their doing it again.

3. Fighting—There are several methods to try with your habitual offenders. They include, but are not limited to, the quiet chair (isolation) during the next fun activity, loss of recess privileges, and punching bag therapy. We generally try to use the quiet chair first.

Ultrasensitivity, left uncontrolled, will nearly always interfere with teaching on-task behaviors.

One disadvantage with the punching bag is that you cannot be sure, with PDD students, whether or not you are teaching them more aggression. Some research has shown punching the bag increases their aggression. We have found that if the children understand that the punching bag is only to be used instead of hitting others, we have more success. However, many crack children will not understand that hitting the bag is all right, but hitting other people is not. That idea may be too abstract for them to comprehend. Caution: If punching the bag escalates aggressive behavior or appears to excite children, immediately take the bag away and do not use it again! If they cannot understand that this is a way to reduce anger or tension, they will most likely get a high from beating on the bag.

4. **Kicking**—Kicking is one of the hardest habits to break with special populations. PDD kids can kick in a heartbeat and move on to the next child before you have even seen them. One method of overcoming this habit is to make kickers lie down on an exercise mat on the floor and kick their legs into the air until they are very tired. That seems to release some of their tension. Since they are not kicking anything but air, they are not learning that it's all right to kick things or people.

5. **Throwing**—Many PDD children are enormously frustrated. Aggressive behavior is one outlet they frequently use to vent their frustration. If they are nonverbal, the aggressive act gives relief to what they are experiencing inside. Their anger, hurt, and frustration builds up in their heads like pressure in a cooker and sooner or later they explode. When their explosion is aggressive, our job is to teach them a more appropriate way to vent their frustration. PDD children throw things the way two-year-olds throw tantrums. For teachers, the problem with throwing is that many times we cannot get near the target quickly enough to deflect the object.

When a child has thrown something, one consequence that can be effective is to not allow the child to play with a ball during recess. However, you must explain that the child cannot play with the ball because he or she threw something inappropriately in the classroom. If the child seems to understand, then the consequence is appropriate. Otherwise try something else. For example isolate the child during play time or another time when throwing an object could occur.

6. **Biting**—There are at least two kinds of biters: the quick-bite artist, who takes a chunk out of you and quickly retreats; and the tenacious biter who locks on to you. With the biter who won't let go, simply press the bitten appendage against the biter's mouth. This movement generally catches the child off-guard and he or she lets go. NEVER pull away! **IF THE SKIN IS BROKEN, SEEK IMMEDIATE MEDICAL TREATMENT.**

The child who bites and runs is more difficult to handle. One suggestion is to make sure that everyone understands "no biting." Any biting incident must be followed by immediate consequences. Say "no biting" and remove the biter to a quiet chair. You might extend the consequences to the loss of a favorite activity. In other words, pair the undesirable behavior with losing a "fun" time. The child's parent or caretaker should be notified **promptly** by you or the school. A discussion of consequences and a clear-cut plan for home involvement should be instituted immediately.

NOTE: Charting triggering events for these aggressive acts will often give you a handle on why the acts occur. Most crack kids cannot explain to you why they lash out. Keeping a simple frequency chart and noting the behaviors that occurred just before an outburst will give you answers more quickly than just trying to observe the aggressor.

E. Changing the Tune

Self-stimulating behaviors are those that "entertain" a child, without anyone else being involved at all. One of the best examples is twirling strings or straws. We had a student who could bring straws out of his pocket already twisting and turning them in between his index finger and thumb. No matter how quickly we removed them from his hands, another would magically appear.

These behaviors are generally looked on as inappropriate, and many of them are not socially acceptable. Most educators immediately think of masturbation when self-stimulating behaviors are mentioned. While socially unacceptable, masturbation is one of the least destructive behaviors that PDD children engage in at school. Of greater concern is being so absorbed in twirling a straw that the child pays no attention to where he or she is walking. Since many crack kids are impervious to pain, they can harm themselves very badly with self-stimulating, self-abusive behaviors. For example, these children may be fascinated with their fingers, bringing them ever closer to their eyes until finally they damage their eyes with the same fingers that fascinated them at first.

Think about self-stimulating behaviors that "normal" people engage in from time to time, like scratching their faces, "popping" their knuckles, or rubbing their necks. These provide a somewhat socially acceptable form of self-stimulating behavior for grown-ups. Biting fingernails to the quick is less acceptable but is done in public compulsively by many "mature" people. PDD children are no different from the majority of us in this respect.

There are several generic interventions you can use when children are self-stimulating inappropriately. Use your own judgment about which one to use when.

Charting triggering events for these aggressive acts will often give you a handle on why the acts occur.

PDD children may be self-abusive and self-stimulatory as long as they cannot find an alternative way to communicate their frustration, sadness, happiness, and anger to the significant people in their world.

1. Distraction—When children are self-stimulating (for example, they are rubbing their noses hard with the heel of their hand), you can ask them to do something for you that requires the use of their hands, preferably something that is not around their face. Let them put up a sign for you, or empty the pencil sharpener. Most PDD children will not understand a philosophical discussion on why they shouldn't spend six hours a day rubbing their noses.

2. Replacement—Put an acceptable behavior in the place of an unacceptable one. For children who repeatedly blow their noses on the sleeves of their sweaters, give them a tissue. Reward them verbally if they use the tissue. For children who don't know how to use a tissue, model the correct use.

3. Physical Action—If a child repeatedly hits his or her head against the desk, you must take physical action. If you have tried verbally redirecting the child and the banging behavior continues, walk over to the desk and lift the child's head. Try to do this in the middle of the downward motion to hit the desk. If the child struggles against your hands and continues to bang the desk, remove the child from the desk. Keep the child standing until calm.

In many instances, PDD kids are self-abusive because they are frustrated. Imagine not being able to tell anyone about the exciting events of your life. Wouldn't it be a horrible feeling not to be able to express honest emotion verbally? PDD children may be self-abusive and self-stimulatory as long as they cannot find an alternative way to communicate their frustration, sadness, happiness, and anger to the significant people in their world.

One girl repeatedly slapped her forehead with her palm as hard an she could. She actually had a deep scar from years of that particular self-stimulating behavior. When she reached our high school program, the teacher took the time to chart what triggered the repeated blow to her forehead and found that she always did it when it was time for math. Further charting showed that she also increased the self-stimulation when she had to choose from the school menu for lunch. The teacher instituted a primary (tangible) reinforcement schedule and successfully lowered the self-stimulatory behaviors.

4. Tangible Reinforcement—Obviously the self-stimulating behaviors are meeting needs PDD children have at a particular moment. Find out what they really like to eat, play, or watch. Pair the "treat" with acceptable behaviors. For instance, if they are "twirlers," catch them not twirling and give them the tangible reinforcer immediately. Reward them in PDD time not yours. See Chapter 7 for more on tangible/intangible reinforcement.

F. Let's Play School

We suppose that an educator's dream class would be one filled with bright, healthy, articulate, and happy children. Of course, they would all have age-appropriate school behaviors, sitting quietly at their desks waiting expectantly for pearls of wisdom to drop from our lips! Little chance of that. If the dream doesn't materialize in your class, make reality better by challenging your kids, crack kids included, to become model students. You are probably thinking, how? Unfortunately, there are no sure-fire methods to instill social skills (manners) in any children.

There **will** be a few fortunate teachers who experience this ideal educational situation. They will have a small group of children who want to learn and parents who reinforce their school experiences at home. The problem is that more educators are attempting to teach children who come from less than ideal homes. As shelter, their apartments are barely adequate, and the housing complex often provides a breeding ground for the proliferation of drugs. Even if an immediate family member is not using drugs, children might see events (drug deals coming down, shootings, gang violence) outside their own door that could change the toughest of us. We know because our own school children tell us daily what horrific event happened at home the night before.

Even very young inner city children may come to school hostile, with little respect for the one concept our society has always claimed sacred—life. They tell us that they don't care what a teacher wants done in the classroom. They continually disrupt by yelling or fighting. They ridicule and resist any attempt at conformity to stated rules. They state flatly that they don't care what you do to them. The truth is that most (not all) kids **do respond** to limits set for them and they **do want** to know what is expected of them by adults.

Inner city children, attending school for the first time, are usually frightened and insecure. Your decision to deal with them (from day one) with honesty and consistency can have a great impact on their street smart minds. **CONSISTENCY OF CONSEQUENCES** from the teacher sets the stage for security for these children. They don't have to worry that one minute you are going to be yelling at them and the next hugging them with sticky sweet words. Your classroom should have set rules (stated in a positive manner), consequences for breaking those rules, and rewards for compliance. You, the classroom teacher, should not take personal offense at the words and actions of these children. In choosing inappropriate behavior, the students only hurt themselves. You, **the teacher**, choose the consequences coolly, identifying those that will benefit each child and hopefully modify future behavior.

CONSISTENCY OF CONSEQUENCES from the teacher sets the stage for security for these children.

45

We have a responsibility as educators to help PDD students achieve as many "normal" developmental milestones as possible.

By now you may be wondering how "normal" kindergartners behave. What exactly does a "normal" kindergartner do? Here's a short list:

1. eat	6. talk	11. fall	16. sit
2. sleep	7. sing	12. scream	17. swing
3. play	8. run	13. color	18. bite
4. laugh	9. fuss	14. cuss	19. catch
5. cry	10. spit	15. cut	20. throw

There are multitudinous things that these neat little creatures can do, and just that many that aren't yet in their repertoire. PDD children can do some of the same things. But these children are not as developmentally advanced as their school-age peers in many areas. The activities listed above are quite simple, yet many of the PDD population can't do them. While that is very sad, it is a fact. We have a responsibility as educators to help PDD students achieve as many "normal" developmental milestones as possible.

Bear in mind, however, that PDD children present unique profiles. We had one five-year-old who understood vocabulary at only a three-year-old level, yet could read on a fourth grade level and recite all the brands of detergent from his local grocery store along with their cost per ounce. His memory skills were phenomenal, but his grasp of the spoken word was minimal. PDD children have many strengths and weaknesses in their little bodies. If we could graph the peaks and valleys, you would be amazed at the range of their skills.

Over the years we have tried many, many ideas to make our PDD students at least appear more normal. Our staff has devoted hundreds of hours to reading, researching, writing, and implementing plan after plan. Some ideas have worked beautifully; others failed miserably.

Here is a compilation of what we have seen work. Take these suggestions and run with them, please!

1. Playground Etiquette—Four, five, and six-year-olds play together on the playground with varying amounts of interaction. They must be closely supervised. Try small group games such as stitch-starch, ring around the rosy, jump the brook, and Mother, may I? Choose one happy-go-lucky peer to play with your withdrawn PDD student. Try not to pair up your "Dennis the Menace" with "Bashful Bobby." Neither of them will have much fun. Encourage your PDD children to play at every recess, even if they play alone. Some of ours will parallel play, but are horrified if we urge them to play with someone. Use your regular education knowledge to work for you with these special children, who are almost guaranteed to have some age appropriate characteristics. Build on them and make sure they have plenty of positive peer models.

2. Secrets—Young children love to whisper, giggle, and blush together. Use that as a jumping off place for your circle time. Play the old-fashioned "gossip" game where you whisper a short sentence into the ear of one of your articulate children and he or she passes it on to the next child, and so on. The children love it and you'll surely get a laugh from the last child's sentence!

3. Parallel Play—At least once a day have a short period of free play for your children. Watch them carefully during the first few days of the school year and see whether or not they interact with anyone else. Use building blocks, foam shapes, cars, trucks, floor puzzles, and other objects to interest them. Add something new every day or two. We try to include different textures, too. One of our teachers will put out beat-up old pots and pans with wooden spoons. Another teacher provides old grown-up clothing and shoes. It's fun to watch all your students with different items, and you learn a great deal about each child.

4. Academic Time—You already know that PDD children are not going to perform on grade level, as a general rule. Once you recognize a child with potential academic difficulties, immediately put that child near you or your paraprofessional. Begin to find out what the child can do. There are many excellent screening devices on the market today. We have tried several and have found them to help us more quickly identify problem areas. (See Chapter 2.)

Many PDD children have gaps in their skill repertoire; they may know how to tell time at age four, but still can't put on their coats without help. Let their high-level skills work for you in the classroom. Use them as a springboard to build new skills. PDD students need all the help they can get. We had one young child who simply refused to speak. He was in our program for two years and had not uttered a word. Then his teacher began taking him to the playground a couple of times a week after school. She would repeatedly sign and say the names of the playground equipment. Soon he began to sign "power" words such as *come, help, stop, yes, play,* and tried to imitate her voice.

5. Music—We manage to salvage many afternoons by turning off the lights, pulling down the blinds, lying on the floor with the children, and playing symphonic music. (We would not suggest the *1812 Overture* for this particular time.) Vivaldi's *Four Seasons* is one of our kids' favorites. One especially nonresponsive child will lie on the floor, hum softly, then even dance occasionally. Try using soft slow music during academics. Drawing and coloring to music is another effective technique. Use music to liven up your students, too. Let them dance around in a frenzy for a few minutes, maybe to a rap or jazz piece. Stop the music and ask them to make a sound that they have just heard. You'll be amazed at what they heard.

> *Many PDD children have gaps in their skill repertoire: let their high-level skills work for you in the classroom. Use them as a springboard to build new skills.*

Every year we have a holiday program, usually at night for parents and then again at a daytime assembly. Our student population is all diagnostically labeled as severely emotionally disturbed, and a fairly large proportion of our students are PDD. Each grade level presents its students in a skit, pantomime, song, or recitation. Many students who do none of those things are there in costume.

Two years ago one of our severely involved autistic children played a reindeer at the show. The child's grandfather started crying as soon as he saw his grandchild on the stage wearing brown paper antlers and bells. Afterwards he told the child's teacher that his grandchild (who was 14 at the time) had never been in anything in his whole life. The next morning the grandfather appeared at school to take the entire class to breakfast.

Musical programs such as these are hard work for everyone involved. However, the kids like performing, the parents love to watch, and the effort pays off, many times over.

6. Ignoring Inappropriate Behavior—If one or more of your PDD children act out during any given part of the day, try ignoring them. If they are out for attention, they will soon stop. Of course, you can't ignore them if they are throwing pencils, slapping children, or screaming at the top of their lungs. If, however, you can move the class to another location, leaving your paraprofessional in charge, do that. If that is not feasible and you can tolerate the misbehavior, you will find that, in most instances, the noise will subside.

We have actually been able to teach whole classes to ignore small, irritating behaviors (like tapping a pencil, sniffing, humming, snapping fingers, "teacher, teacher"). We offer transitional reinforcers (See Chapter 7) to the children who ignore the inappropriate behaviors. You can shape the response of the normal population in your class by using the following method:

A. When one or more students are behaving inappropriately, say to a "good" child: "Wow! _____, I really like the way you are sitting quietly waiting for your clay. You may choose a treasure from our special chest."

B. The very instant one of the guilty ones behaves appropriately say: "_____, you surely did get quiet quickly. Here's a sticker for changing your behavior." Do not give the same reinforcer that you gave to the first child.

C. If the others continue to misbehave, simply go on as though they weren't there. When it is time for the next activity (which should be a fun one) say: "_____, _____, and _____, please go to the quiet chair (corner). You have lost the privilege of finger painting today. I hope you can make a better choice and be with us the rest of the day." This may not always work, but it is certainly worth a try.

In Chapter 2, we have listed several how-to books we have found useful in planning classroom activities and molding behavior. Don't hesitate to try your own methods; your ideas are just as valid as anyone else's. If chefs didn't experiment with different ingredients, we'd probably never have gotten so many kinds of cheesecake!

4 Communicating means more than talking

Since most PDD kids have reduced language skills, frustration or aggression always seems to be their first communication option...

When we talk about a child's verbal skills, the most important question to answer must be, how well does the child communicate? The concern should not be whether a child can use words to talk to you, but if he or she can communicate well enough to convey physical needs, feelings (emotions) about current and future events, and ideas. If a child is nonverbal, then consideration must be given to alternative forms of communication such as gestures, sign language, a communication board, wallet pictures, or even a computer-assisted voice synthesizer. There are many wonderful augmentative programs on the market to assist special children in having a little control in their world. It has been proven time and time again that there is a strong correlation between level of communicative competency and behavior; the more skilled children are in expressing themselves, the happier and better self-controlled they are, behaviorally, in most situations. When children improve their verbal repertoire, there is usually a decrease in inappropriate behavior. This certainly does not infer that the behavior is angelic, but it will improve in most children. Children who have enough vocabulary to state their position are less likely to react physically. Since most PDD kids have reduced language skills, frustration or aggression always seems to be their first communication option when they can't let us know what they want or feel.

Speech and language delays are common occurrences with children prenatally exposed to drugs. These delays can result from many factors, but the most probable causes are the physical/health problems that such infants have to fight first, just for survival. Seizures, abnormally formed internal organs, rapid heart rate, abnormal sucking and swallowing, low birth weight, impaired motor development, an overly sensitive sensory feedback system, and difficulty sleeping are just a few of the problems these infants must conquer even before the candle has been blown out on their first birthday cake.

The physical impairments also carry over into mental and emotional abnormalities such as: unresponsiveness, irritability, disorientation, poor interactive capacities, frequent momentary shocks (being startled), poor processing skills, difficulty being calmed, and alterations in bonding and attachment. Children who have difficulty bonding cannot feel the security they need to reach out to the world they must explore and begin to understand. These terrified children begin a journey into a wilderness of stimulus information indecipherable to them. The world makes no sense, and confusion only seems to grow worse with each passing hour.

Language/vocabulary development must be the tool we use to bring order and reason into their lives. Any regular or special education classroom is packed to capacity with language. Every single thing you do from lining up for lunch (in front, behind, wait, stop, tickets, next, tray, milk, fork, etc.) to doing an art activity (cut, scissors, color, construction paper, lines, draw, glue, pretty) is filled with vocabulary that is important to each child. The more new words/concepts you can introduce and use repeatedly, the better for all your children. When you introduce a new idea, use it not only that day, but the next and repeatedly throughout the year. Ask questions about the concept and let the children explain to you what it means. The more you use a word/concept in different contexts, the more likely it is that the idea will stick.

One teaching concept that has been used by special educators for years is now being incorporated into the regular classroom. The "whole language" or thematic approach is fast gaining acceptance. (Goodman, 1986). This philosophy stresses that the same vocabulary/ concepts be taught in all the academic subjects. Thus, throughout the day, instead of segmenting instruction under specific headings with different concepts being taught in each discipline, the same concepts are taught in each subject area. Reading, science, spelling, math, social studies, art, and even music will use the same vocabulary/concepts. (Example: Transportation—for reading you would teach the different types of transportation by using textbooks, magazines, storybooks, encyclopedias. In science, you would teach the mechanical aspects: pulleys, levers, engines, generators. Spelling could be teaching the spelling of all the transportation words. For math you could count all the vehicles. In social studies you could study how transportation affects our lives. In art the children could make a train and in music the children could sing, *The Wheels on the Bus*.)

The proponents of this type of teaching feel that language is not learned by analyzing and repetitiously teaching concepts and skills. Learning is achieved by bombardment, just as a child learns at home prior to entering kindergarten. We realize that this is a very simplistic analysis of this philosophy, so you will need to read your latest educational journals for more detailed explanations. This method of teaching does not require the purchasing of a new kit or program, simply a change in the way you view learning. We feel a whole language program approach has a great deal of merit and deserves your consideration.

This chapter is devoted to a basic explanation of language acquisition, alternative forms of communication (gestures, sign language, communication boards, wallet pictures, etc.), and how important communication is to socialization.

The more you use a word/concept in different contexts, the more likely it is that the idea will stick.

We must address the prerequisite skills children must learn before we can expect them to exhibit age-appropriate behaviors.

A. Talk It Up!

What is language and why is it so important? Language is a systematic clustering of gestures, body postures, facial expressions, and sounds which, when combined, denote the names/words of everything around us, including persons, places, things, actions, feelings, ideas. Among the multiple reasons that one human being uses language to communicate with another human being are: to have physical needs met (food, water, shelter); to be comforted; to be entertained; to direct another person's behavior; to get help; and for finding a partner. Each language is understood by all members of a specific group of people. For each child to be accepted into this autonomous group, he or she must learn the subtleties required for that particular language system.

Pervasively developmentally delayed kids do not easily decipher the secret language code, placing them on the outer edge of social acceptability. For example, we take our PDD students to the mall regularly. These children may grab anything and everything in sight. Usually one of us will eventually be on the floor in the middle of the mall, restraining an out-of-control child. This child cannot communicate to us a desire for cotton candy so he or she screams and emits guttural sounds. Surrounding us are adults who, although trained not to stare, nevertheless stand absolutely still with their jaws dropped, as they watch.

As we look at kids who are developmentally delayed, we must address the prerequisite skills children must learn before we can expect them to exhibit age-appropriate behaviors. Just look at a developmental chart to learn all the steps that are missing in a child who is five years old chronologically, but who functions as a two- or three-year-old. Prizant (1991) identified the following as Early Symptomatology for Children who are at risk for impaired social and communication development (first year of life):

1. Lack of responsiveness to sounds
2. Lack of social smile
3. Absence of conventional pre-verbal communication
4. Limited reciprocity in vocalization and action
5. Difficulty in engaging in social games
6. Peculiarities of gaze; behavior-gaze aversion or staring empty
7. Diminished or monotonic repetitive vocalizations
8. Attachment to select objects
9. Failure to anticipate social approaches

Many studies have been done on two-year-olds that identify children most likely to develop language/learning problems. In addition to the characteristics described by Prizant, these studies have identified others:

1. Poor or nonexistent gestures even before age two (or use of lots of gestures instead of speech)
2. Lack of age-appropriate vocabulary (does not understand receptive speech)
3. Deficient nonverbal skills (eye contact, facial expressions, body posture)
4. Large vocabulary but short utterances (one or two words)
5. Difficulty understanding what is told to them
6. Continually displaying frustration when they are not understood

Since we can expect children with these characteristics to be deficient, early diagnosis is imperative for effective intervention, prior to entering school. Once these children enter school, they are immediately identifiable because they are so different from the majority of your class.

Early diagnosis is imperative for effective intervention, prior to entering school.

> Tony entered the kindergarten room on the first day of school, and Mrs. Leslie, the teacher, knew immediately something was wrong. He stood immobile exactly where his mother had put him. Tony didn't even cry when his mother left. As a matter of fact, he did nothing but swing the broken earpiece of a pair of sunglasses back and forth in front of his face. When Mrs. Leslie attempted to turn him toward the play area, he began screaming without tears, but didn't say a word. She tried to touch him to calm him, but the screaming changed to warbling sounds until she let him go. The moment she stopped touching him, his face lost all expression. He put the broken sunglasses back in front of his face and he again began to sway. This behavior continued for at least twenty minutes until he was placed in a chair. Tony didn't resist being placed in the chair, but he immediately jumped up and ran out the door. If he had not been so uncoordinated, the teacher would not have been able to catch him. When Mrs. Leslie turned his face toward her to get eye contact, he quickly averted his eyes and he began to scream again without tears, but this time he added kicking and hitting to his behaviors. When Tony's mother arrived later at the school, her only comment about his behavior was that he "just don't talk and he might need extra help."

This is just one example of what a regular classroom teacher seems to be facing more and more. Pressure has increased, because of funding constraints and parental pressure, to place special children into regular classrooms. We have seen great progress made in behavior, academics, socialization, and communication when handicapped children are placed even part-time in a regular education classroom. However, we have also seen the placement of a handicapped child interfere with the learning of the other children to such an extent that the special child had to be removed. We advocate equal and appropriate education for all children, but not to the detriment of either group. We feel the best solution must be the addition of support staff to the classroom. The reality, however, is that this does not happen often.

B. Let's Make a Connection

A child who has been prenatally exposed to drugs is often born with damage to the central nervous system, including the brain. Crack and other drugs have been shown to damage acetylcholine, the neurotransmitter chemical required for normal brain cell firings. This defect is obvious when you ask a prenatally drug exposed child a question. You may get either no response or one that is so off topic it will make you laugh. It's as if the question got only halfway to its destination and stopped, or somehow the question was sent to the wrong long-term memory location.

Unfortunately, neurologists, psychologists, speech/language specialists, and behaviorists do not fully understanding how even the normal brain works. For example, what makes one event stick around in the brain for only a few seconds in short-term memory, but another event remain forever in long-term memory? Until a more complete picture of normal brain functioning is available, we are not likely to make any headway in understanding and correcting the damaged functioning of a crack kid's brain. It is, however, possible to partially overcome the defect and achieve some level of function.

Many PDD children retain language information in their short-term memory only. This is not learning. That's why they can do three addition problems after explanation on Tuesday, but on Wednesday they have no idea even where to begin. In most cases, with repetition, PDD children will suddenly understand how to do those addition problems every day because their brains will develop the necessary neural pathways for long-term memory. Neural pathways are the tracks the "brain train" runs on between the "stations" called neural processes, which are pockets that serve as "holding tanks" for information.

Crack/cocaine, and other drugs can affect emotional stability since acetylcholine also transmits specific feelings. A normal child seems to have equalizing valves for emotions such as pleasure and aversion; calmness and rage; and excitement and depression. Once the emotion valve is opened on a neurologically damaged child, there doesn't seem to be a way to turn it off. Compared to non-PDD kids, the emotional responses of PDD children are basic, extreme, instantaneous, and prolonged.

In most cases, with repetition, PDD children will suddenly understand how to do those addition problems every day because their brains will develop the necessary neural pathways for long-term memory.

The bright spot on the horizon is the recuperative power of a child's brain. Whereas an adult brain may improve only slightly after an injury, a child's brain is a miracle of regenerative neural pathways. Both hemispheres of the brain can be utilized for learning academic material and socially acceptable responses to daily situations.

Let's review briefly how the left and right hemispheres of the brain work as specialized information centers. If you are right-handed, the information you retrieve comes mainly from the left hemisphere of the brain. This multipurpose left hemisphere handles speech, reading, writing, calculation, and hand control. It is the main language center, judging time and sequence. It even processes some of the data arriving from the senses. What all this boils down to is that all the words you are currently reading are mainly understood in the left hemisphere.

The right hemisphere is no slouch either. If you are left-handed, your processing of information comes mainly from the right hemisphere, which is the main area for analyzing most sensory information. This part of the brain recognizes faces, perceives, and organizes spatial orientation. It synchronizes movements and melodies so you can learn to play a Mozart masterpiece. The right side of the brain seems to incorporate the fine arts talents. There is an old theory that left-handed people have an artistic flare. One author of this book is left-handed, and she is musically and vocally talented. So if you're left handed, stick to the theory; if you're right-handed, like a majority of the population, then just say it's another old story that has no meaning. There are many talented right-handed people, largely because of the corpus collosum. This is the large bridge that connects the left and right brain hemispheres, rapidly carrying information back and forth between the hemispheres. Combined, the left and right hemispheres work in concert for virtually all mental processes.

Acquiring language is one of the most fundamental and important intellectual tasks carried out by the brain. Children are born with an innate knowledge of the formal principles of language. This information is genetically prerecorded just as the flying instinct is in a bird. Birds just have to learn to strengthen their wings, and then take short flights until they are perfection in motion. A child must practice, through trial and error, sound combinations and actions until finally the words or skills are perfectly synchronized. Learning, then, is the relationship of the connections between neural pathways (tracks) and processes (stations). From the most simple to the most complex phenomena, there must be an integration of the modalities (the senses) to process the information. Therefore, learning for memory only occurs when there is a mixture of sensory stimulation.

Extremely bright children have a more advanced/matured network of neural pathways. They seem to develop a knowledge base of neural processes which quickly and efficiently integrates new knowledge with old. Their cognitive processes interconnect continuously, using a myriad of formats to analyze, organize, and critique incoming data. We think of the brain's neural pathways as being like KUDZU*, continually growing and intertwining at incredible speed. A pervasively developmentally delayed child's brain is growing, but the process is slower, the pathways are harder to form, and the connectors to neural processes are sometimes broken and not as solid.

The flow chart on the following page shows how communication is a culmination of steps:

1. Starting with an external sensory stimulus
2. Holding the stimulus in short term memory
3. Applying all the language from long term memory (verbal and nonverbal)
4. Coming up with a concept or thought
5. Analyzing the emotions required (self-control, motivation)
6. Comparing the response to the external sensory input for compatibility
7. Communication occurs

*KUDZU — vine-like plant which was imported to the southern U.S. from Japan to help control soil erosion in the 20s. It grows quickly, engulfing everything in its path—trees, telephone poles, old dilapidated houses, and you, if you stand still. Considered by most southerners to be unkillable, it returns year after year with a vast interconnected root system. Suddenly, in the spring, it's everywhere and eternal.

How We Communicate
The Communication Train

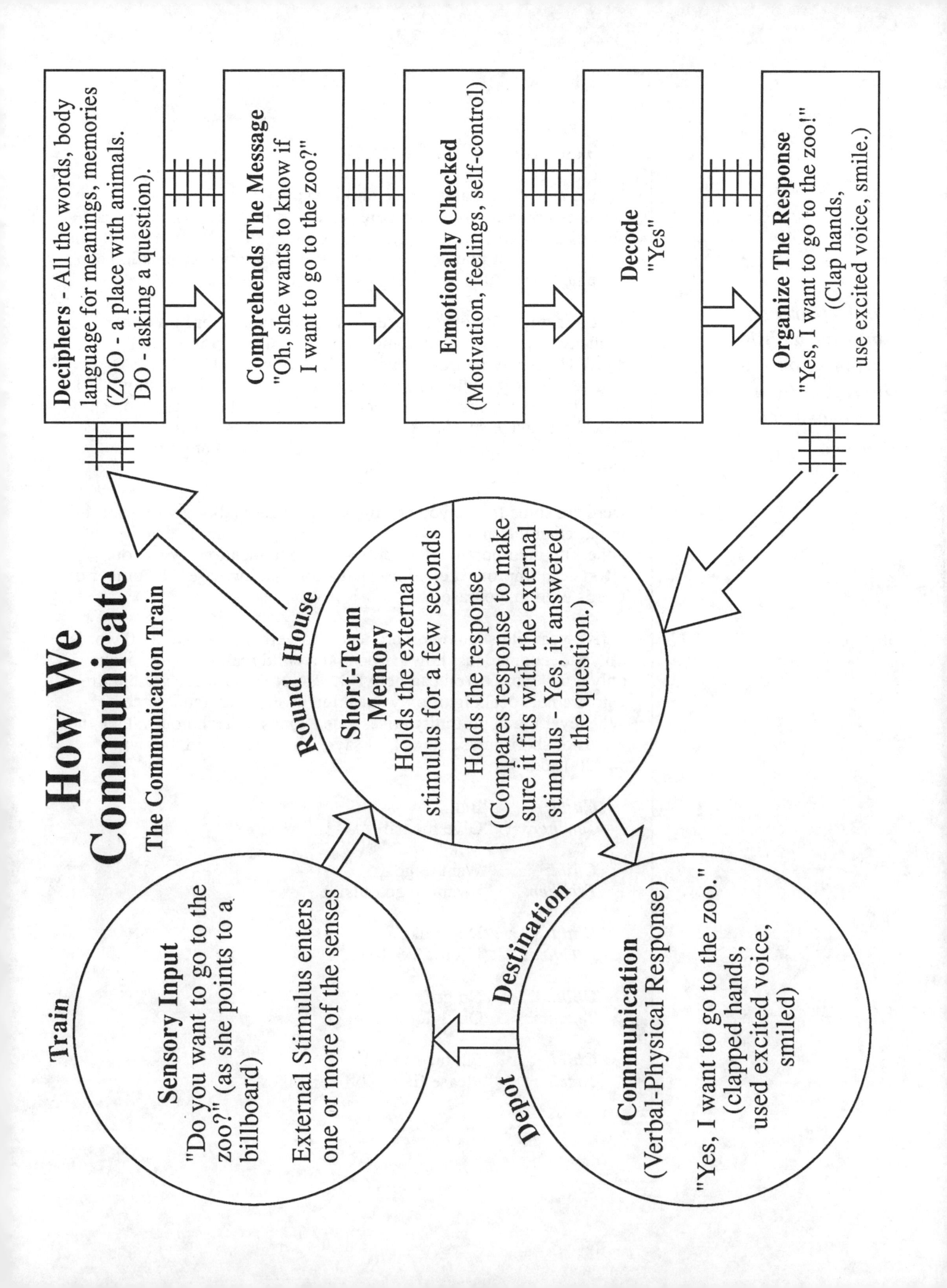

Train

Sensory Input
"Do you want to go to the zoo?" (as she points to a billboard)

External Stimulus enters one or more of the senses

Round House

Short-Term Memory
Holds the external stimulus for a few seconds

Holds the response (Compares response to make sure it fits with the external stimulus - Yes, it answered the question.)

Deciphers - All the words, body language for meanings, memories (ZOO - a place with animals. DO - asking a question).

Comprehends The Message
"Oh, she wants to know if I want to go to the zoo?"

Emotionally Checked
(Motivation, feelings, self-control)

Decode
"Yes"

Organize The Response
"Yes, I want to go to the zoo!" (Clap hands, use excited voice, smile.)

Destination

Depot

Communication
(Verbal-Physical Response)

"Yes, I want to go to the zoo." (clapped hands, used excited voice, smiled)

C. Too Much…Too Little Talk

By the age of five, an average child is spontaneously saying sentences of eight to ten or more words. Most of the child's vocal sounds are perfected, and grammar is almost like that of an adult. In other words, you should be able to have a lengthy conversation and have no trouble understanding anything the child says.

If you feel the child has a speech problem, then refer him or her immediately to the speech/language specialist in your school. A child who is having trouble with articulation (sound errors in words); fluency (stuttering); voice differences (harsh, breathy, soft); or language (communication, academics) should be evaluated. The speech/language specialist can give you all kinds of needed information to help you understand the extent of that particular child's delays.

Here are some things you can do when you are talking with speech-impaired children to provide a model for them to imitate and hopefully incorporate into their own communication style. Your efforts can improve a child's articulation and increase the number of words used in a phrase.

Your efforts can improve a child's articulation and increase the number of words used in a phrase.

A five-year-old should comprehend and verbalize about 2000 words. So you recognize just how far behind a child really is who speaks only a few words. You can help E X P A N D the speech of children who are not speaking or only speaking in short utterances. Whenever the opportunity arises, use expansion techniques: take the words or short phrases the child says, and repeat them, but with word(s) added.

Child: "Ball."
Teacher: "Give me ball."

Child: "Want to go."
Teacher: "I want to go outside."

Child: "Don't like."
Teacher: "I don't like liver."

Child: "No go."
Teacher: "Oh, I don't want go."

Child: "Fix broke bike."
Teacher: "Please fix my broken bike."

Here are some general guidelines for expansion:

Child says:	Expand to:
1 word	2 or 3 words
2 words	3 or 4 words
3 words	4 or 5 words
4 words	5, 6, or 7 words
5 words	7, 8, or more words

An expansion technique is a simple non-intrusive method that will not interfere with the give-and-take of normal conversation. Always remember to add your comments after you have expanded the child's phrases. Try to encourage/acknowledge any attempt at communication, even if the answer to the child's statement must be "no."

Child: "Give block"
Teacher: "Make Kristi give blocks. I know you want blocks, but Kristi's turn."

Undoubtedly, you noticed the articles, conjunctions, and other filler words were left out. Filler words should only be emphasized when a child speaks in phrases of three or more words.

While it is important that you model and expand children's phrases, it is also imperative that you reduce the number (length) of direction words you speak. Suppose you have a PDD child, "Bobby," in your class who seems to be about age three years developmentally. Your verbal directions must be compressed for his developmental age. So when you say, "Bobby, I told you to leave that box alone. Get in your chair. You are not following directions again. If you don't do your writing you will lose recess time. Now get to work," actually what Bobby understands is "Bobby *buzz buzz buzz* box *buzz. Buzz Buzz* chair. *Buzz buzz* work," All the words you are yelling/saying are lost because there is too much information.

We have seen classroom teachers talking on and on at PDD children, when an observer can see how confused, turned off, and hurt they appear. It does no good to rant and rave for several minutes at PDD children because they simply will tune you out or they won't understand all the vocabulary words. A more effective way to talk for understanding is to be very specific using fewer words to convey your commands. "Bobby stop! Sit in chair! Do your writing!" Yes, raise your voice, if necessary to get attention, but then drop the volume to a firm speaking tone. Notice again that the little filler words were left out. They are not necessary for conveying specific classroom instructions. The directions should be short enough for the child to comprehend and long enough to be used as an expansion model. Children do understand repeated, short, simple directions.

Your verbal directions must be compressed for his developmental age... Be very specific using fewer words to convey your commands. "Bobby stop! Sit in chair! Do your writing!"

A wonderful multisensory approach for classroom instruction would be to use verbal instruction, hand signs/gestures, and the printed direction words. The children can hear the message and see both a visual hand sign, and the printed word.

D. Using Our Hands

Sign language has been a proven tool for enhancing the understanding of information/language/directions in the classroom. The literature is full of research stating conclusively that the more senses you address, the more apt the child is to understand what is going on and to comply with your requests.

There may be children in your classroom who do not speak or understand English well enough to participate in the activities you present. If your system does not have ESL support, you must rely heavily on using formal signing as well as gestures and body language to communicate.

A peer can be utilized to support and guide the child through each activity. The child may not understand the language spoken, but can observe another child's reaction to the teacher's instruction. The child does not have to know the word "red" to color in a worksheet.

We have chosen the system, Signing Exact English (SEE), because of its universal acceptance. The signs we have included in this section are for the classroom setting. If there are certain words/signs you need, then just look in your local library. Most of the signs shown here are the words you already verbalize in your classroom. They will help you instruct and control children's behavior throughout the day. Of course, these cannot begin to be inclusive, but at least the list will give you a starting point. When you sign, use your entire body to convey the meaning (for example, frown when you speak/sign "Stop!"). Often a few words convey a more powerful message than talking on and on about the same subject. Since even your PDD kids understand many nonverbal cues, you should be using your hands along with your words.

The following pages illustrate these signs. We hope you'll make helping hands a habit!

> *Research states conclusively that the more senses you address, the more apt the child is to understand what is going on and to comply with your requests.*

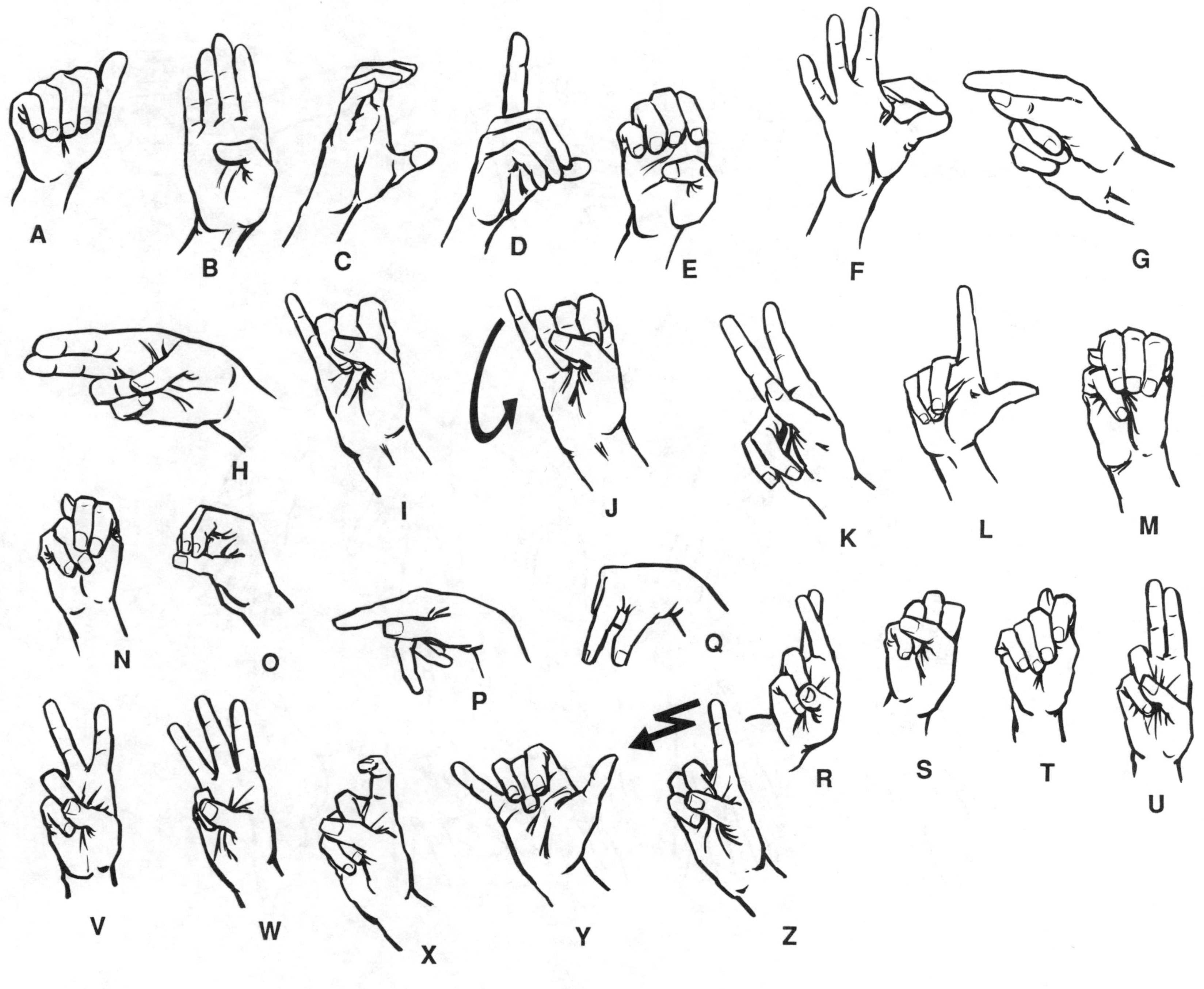
A
B
C
D
E
F
G
H
I
J
K
L
M
N
O
P
Q
R
S
T
U
V
W
X
Y
Z

1 2 3 4 5

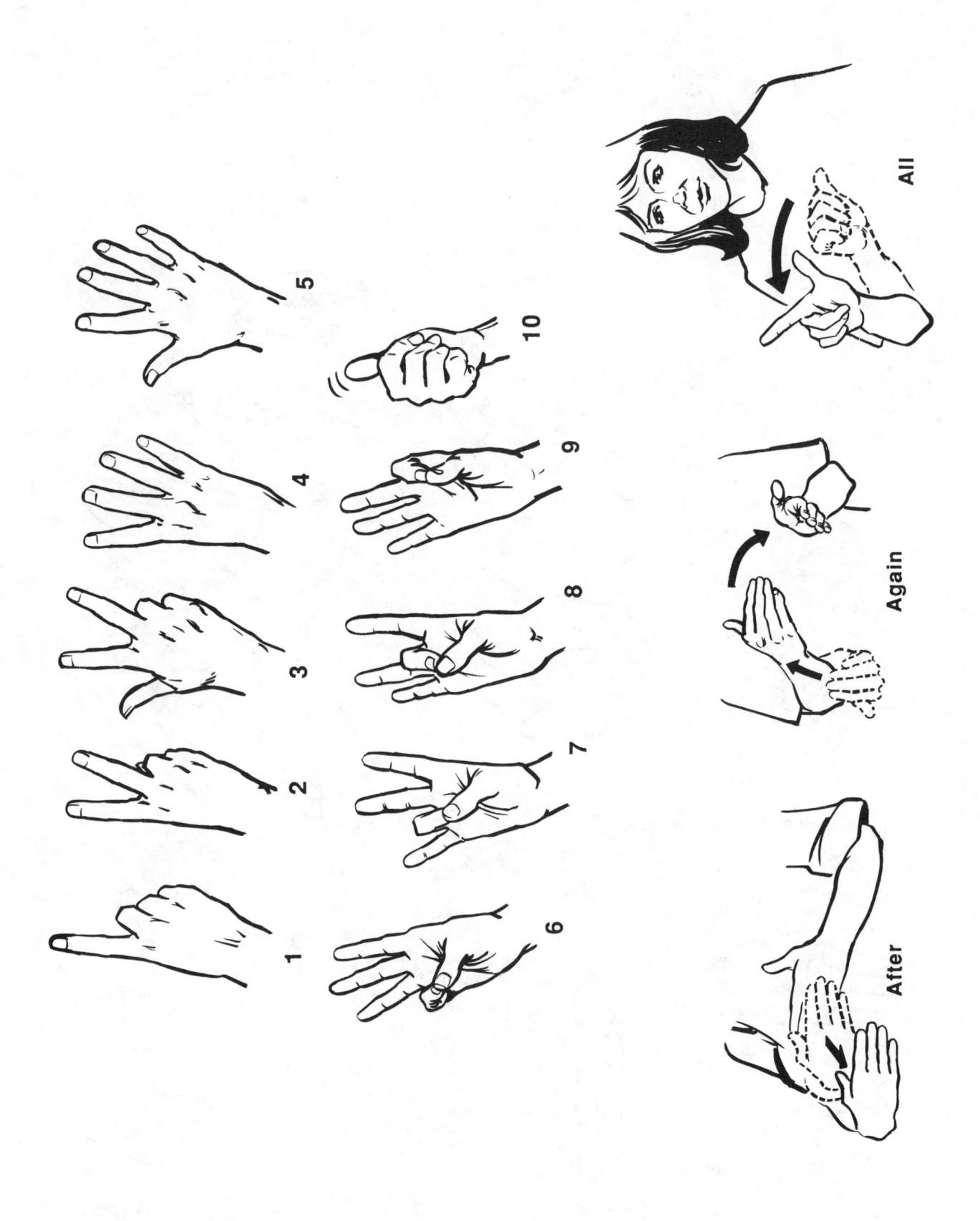

6 7 8 9 10

After

Again

All

Before

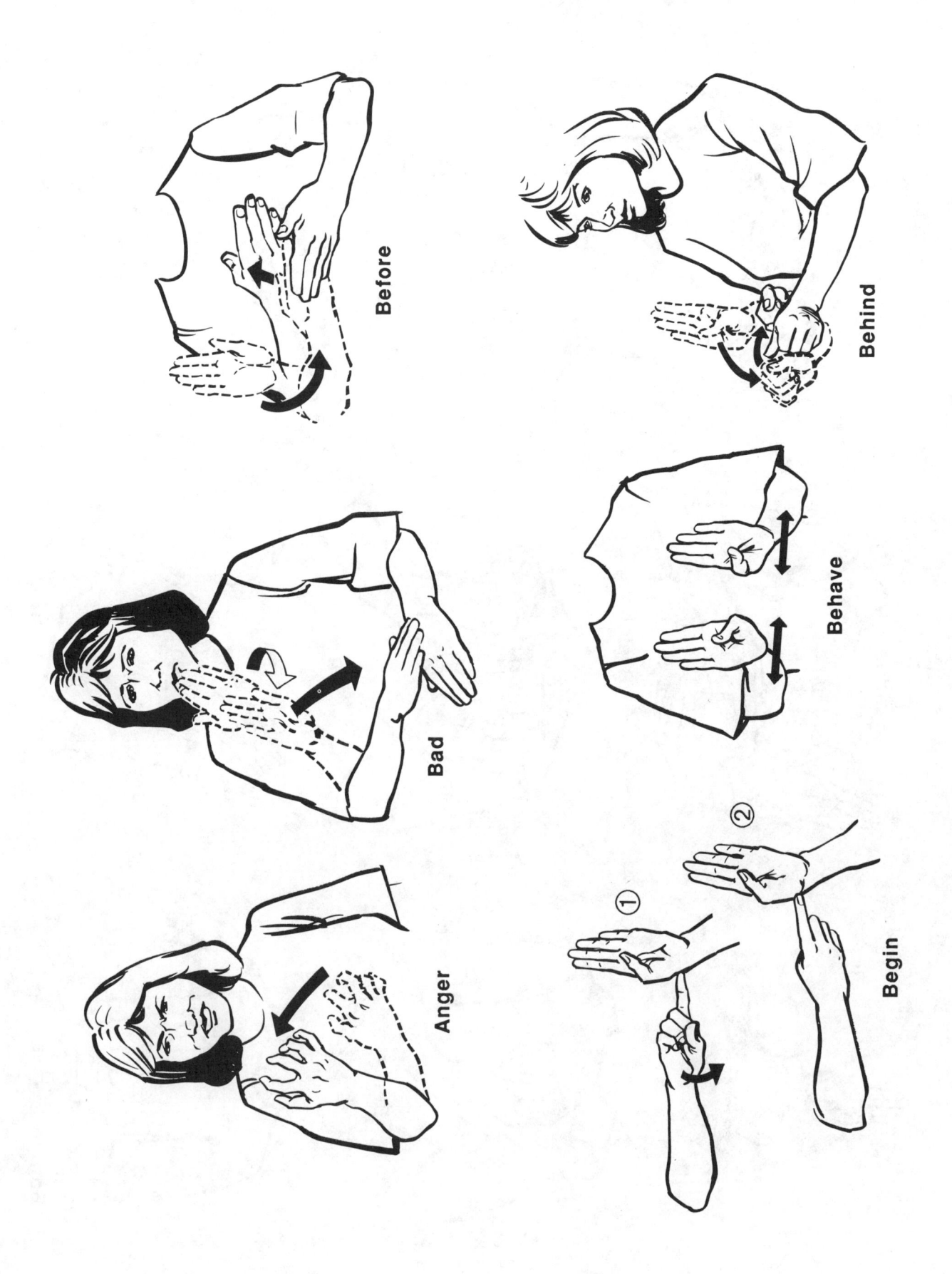

Behind

Bad

Behave

Anger

Begin

Better

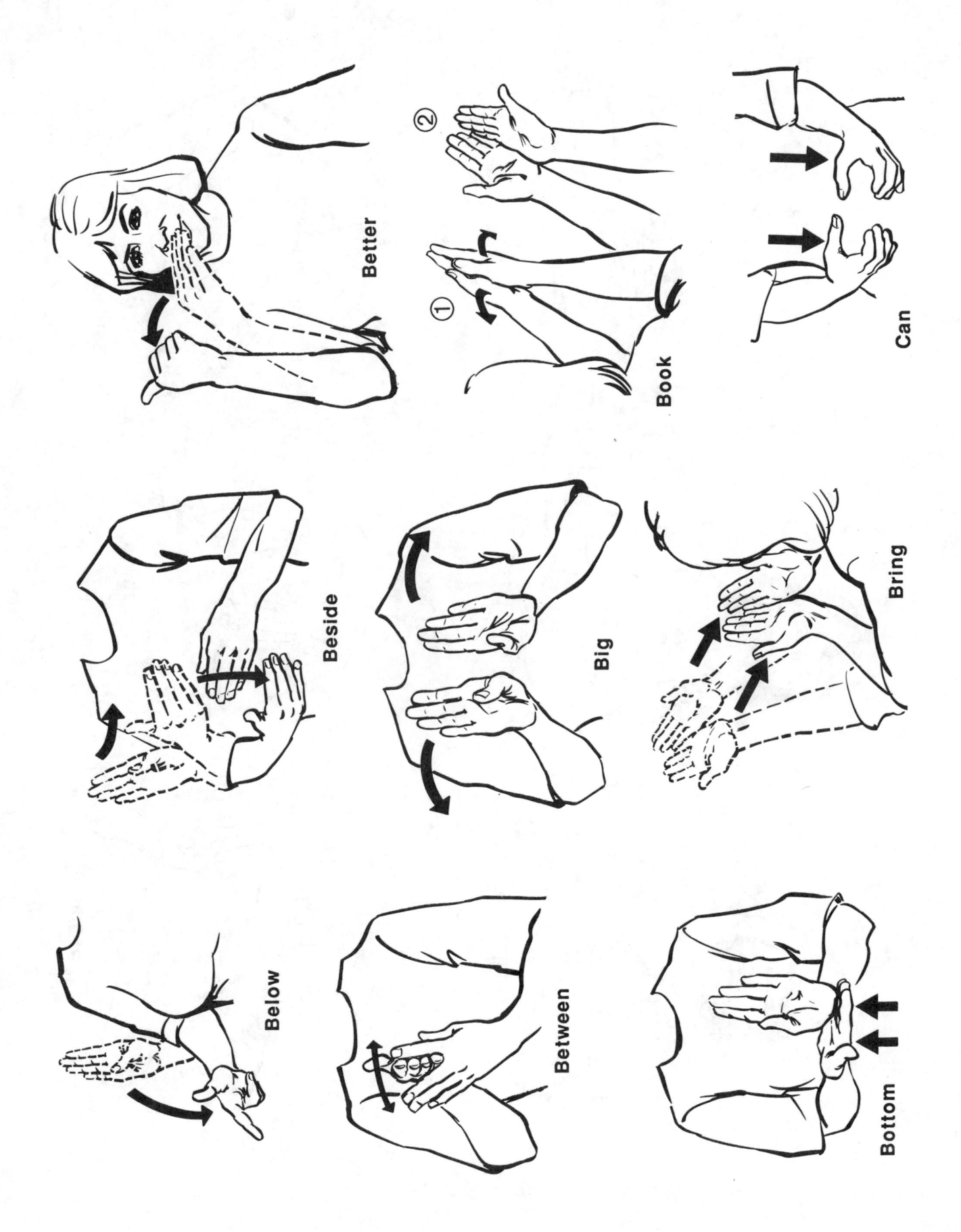

Book

Can

Beside

Big

Bring

Below

Between

Bottom

Class

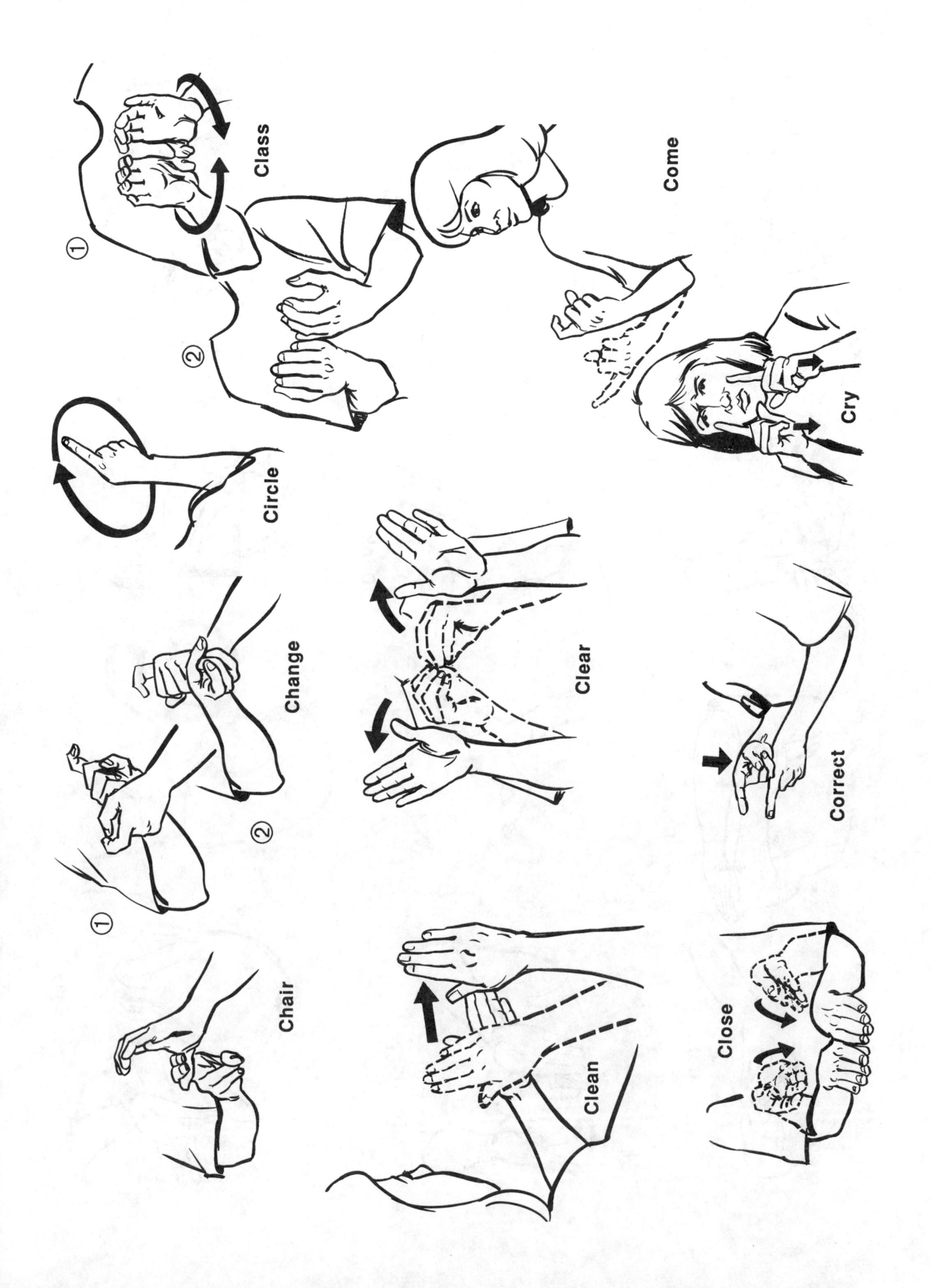

Come

Cry

Circle

Change

Clear

Correct

Chair

Clean

Close

Cut | Desk | Different | Do

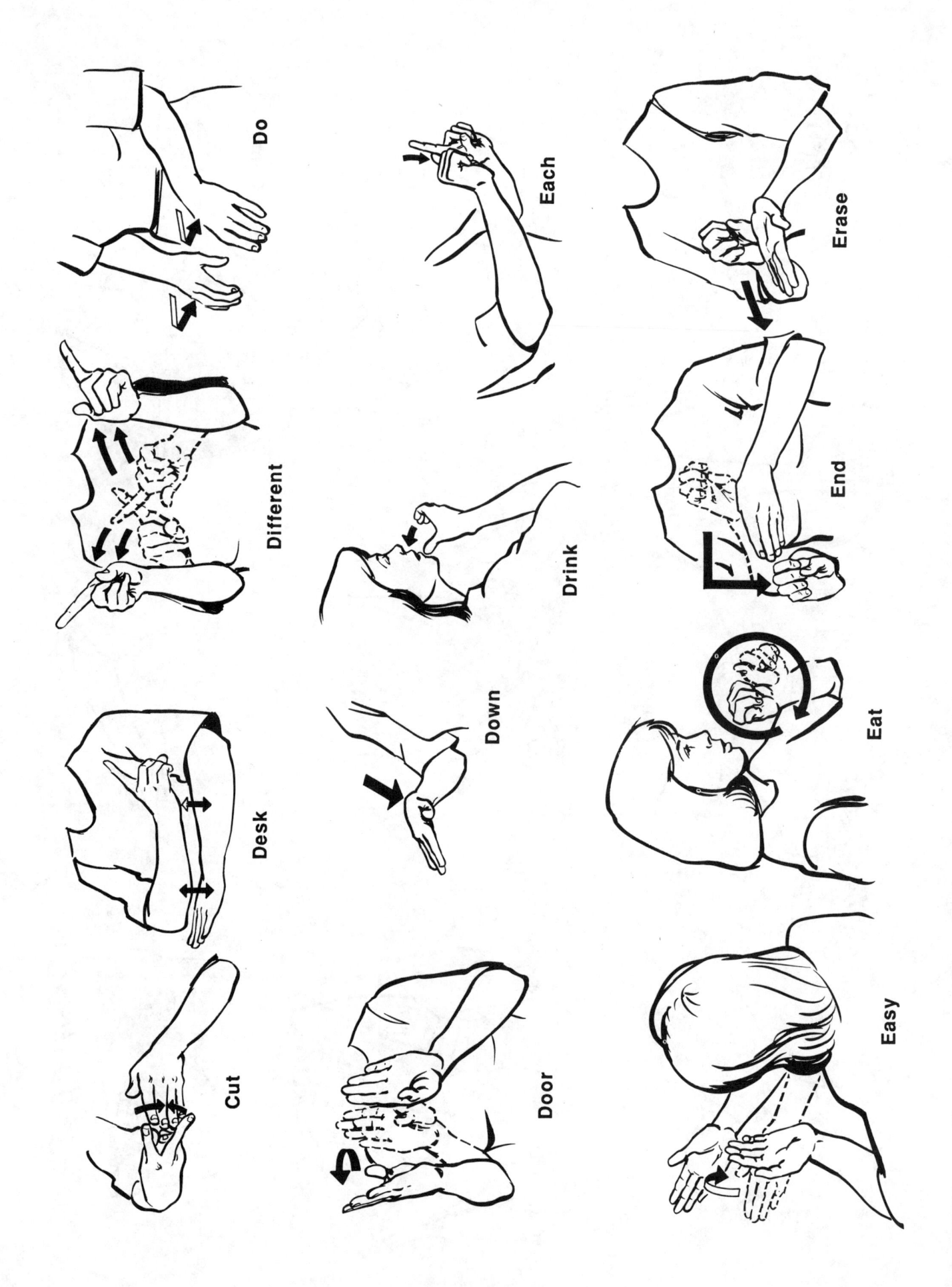

Door | Down | Drink | Each

Easy | Eat | End | Erase

Finish

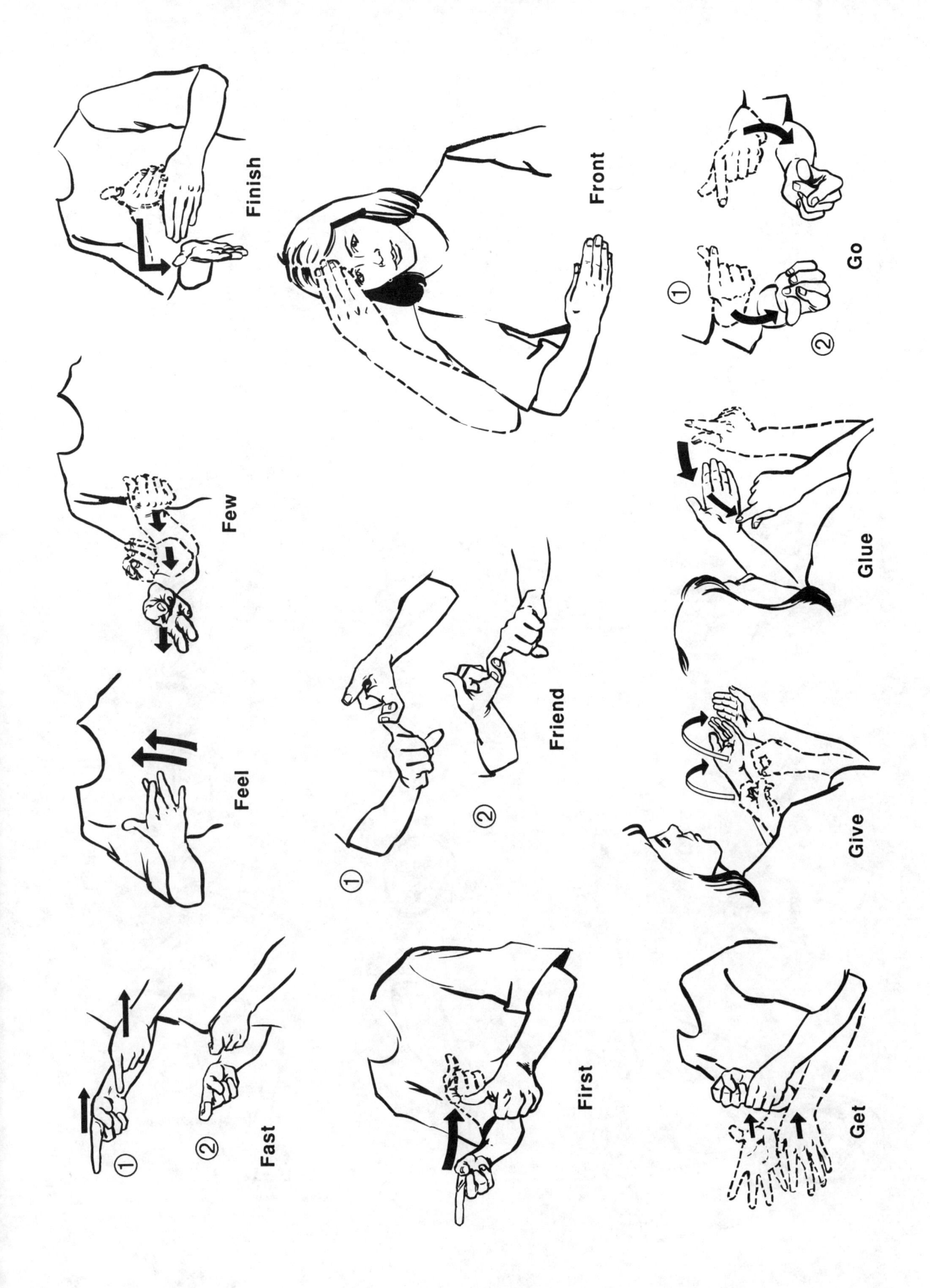

Front

Go

Few

Glue

Feel

Friend

Give

Fast

First

Get

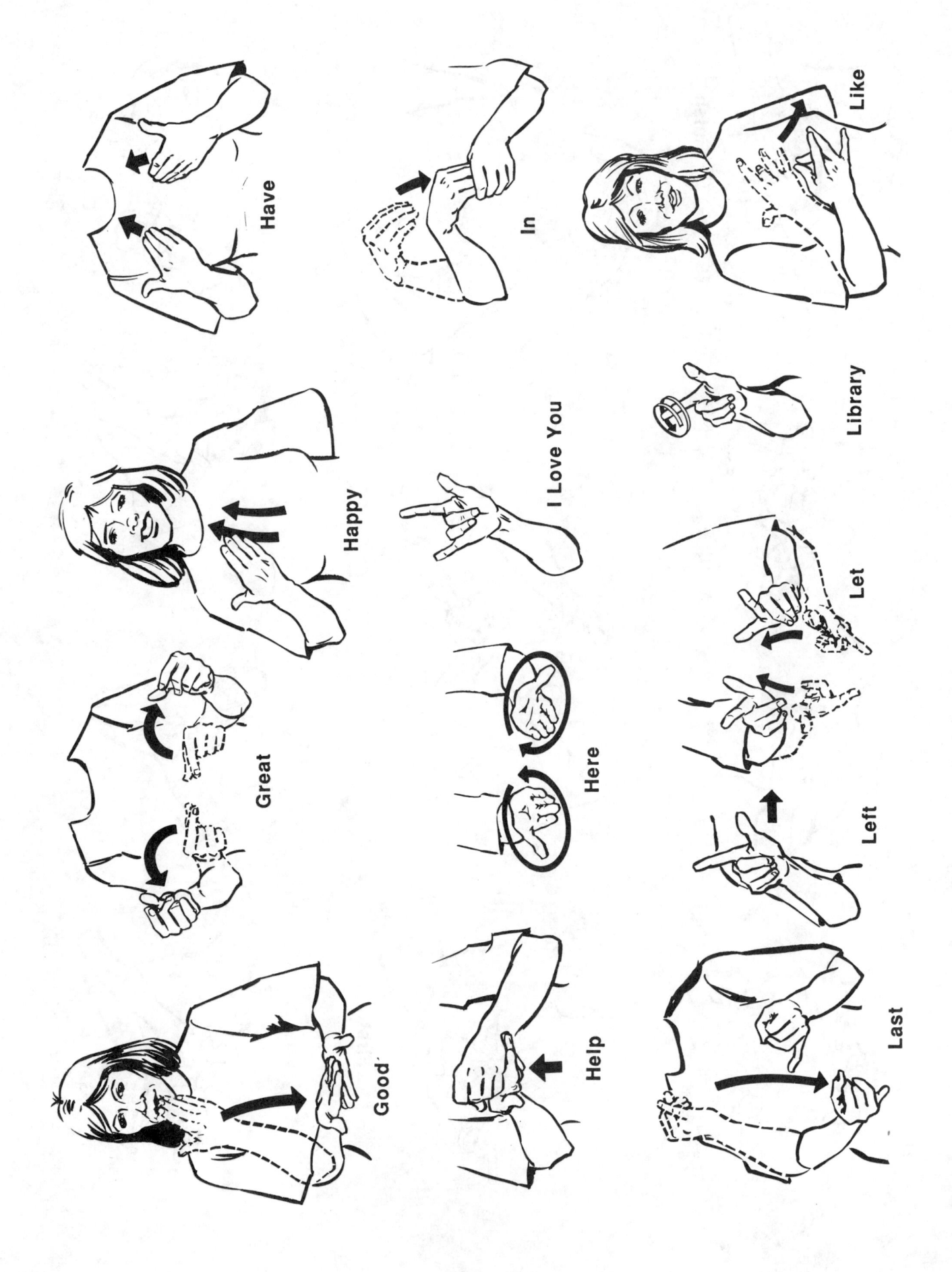

- Have
- In
- Like
- Happy
- I Love You
- Library
- Great
- Here
- Let
- Left
- Good
- Help
- Last

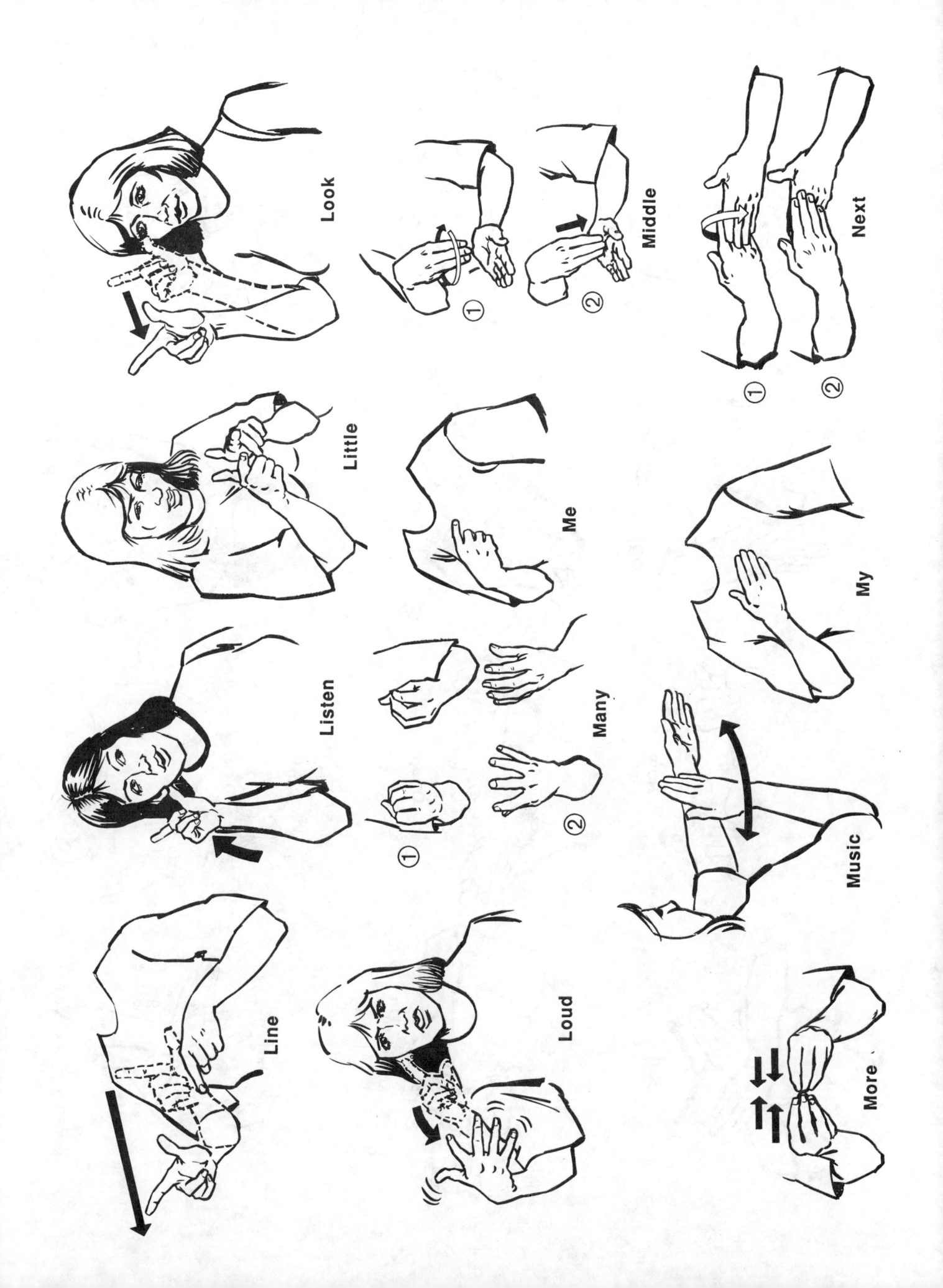

- Look
- Middle
- Next
- Little
- Me
- My
- Listen
- Many
- Music
- Line
- Loud
- More

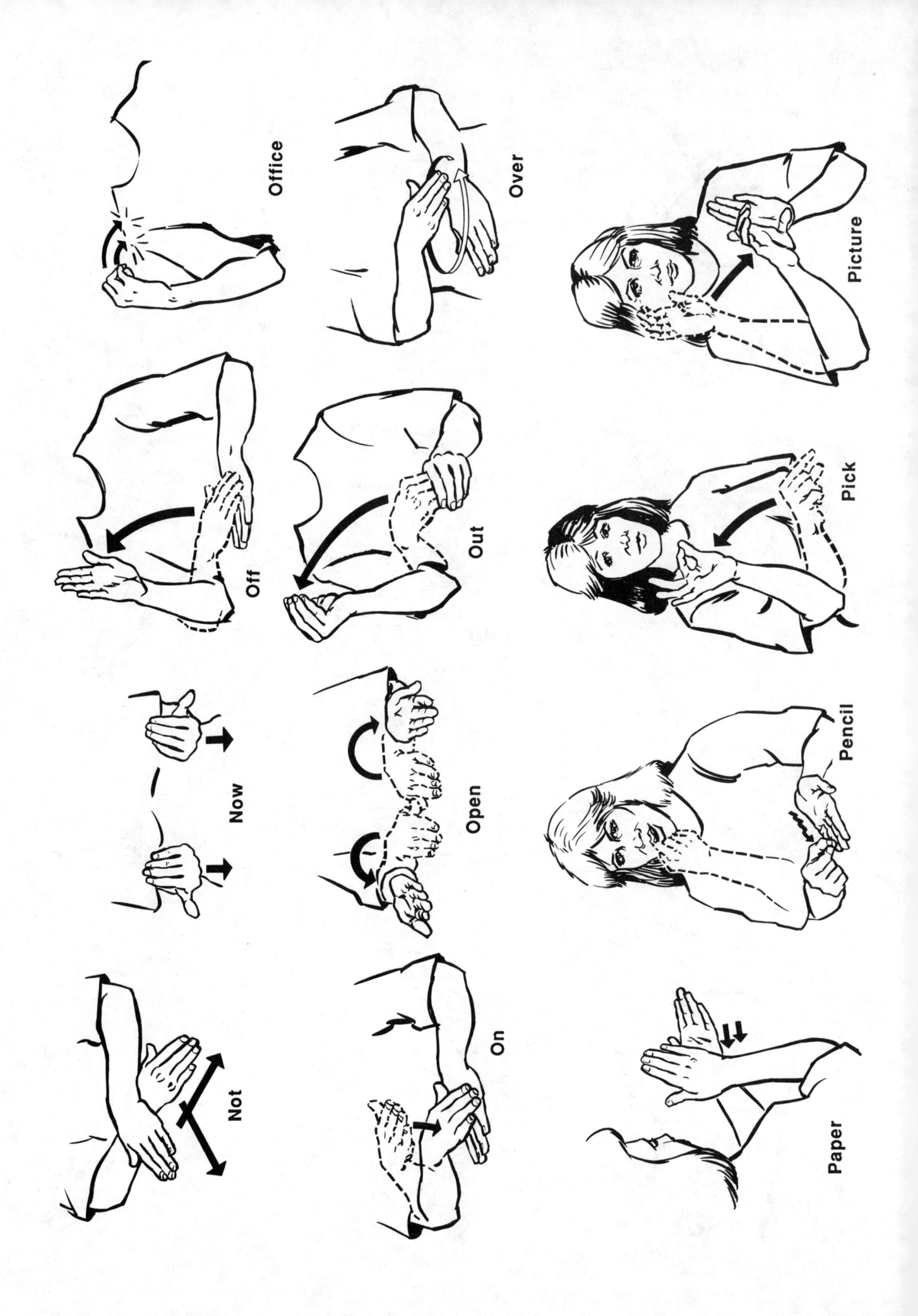

Not	Now	Off	Office
On	Open	Out	Over
Paper	Pencil	Pick	Picture

Quick · Principal · Sad · Shut

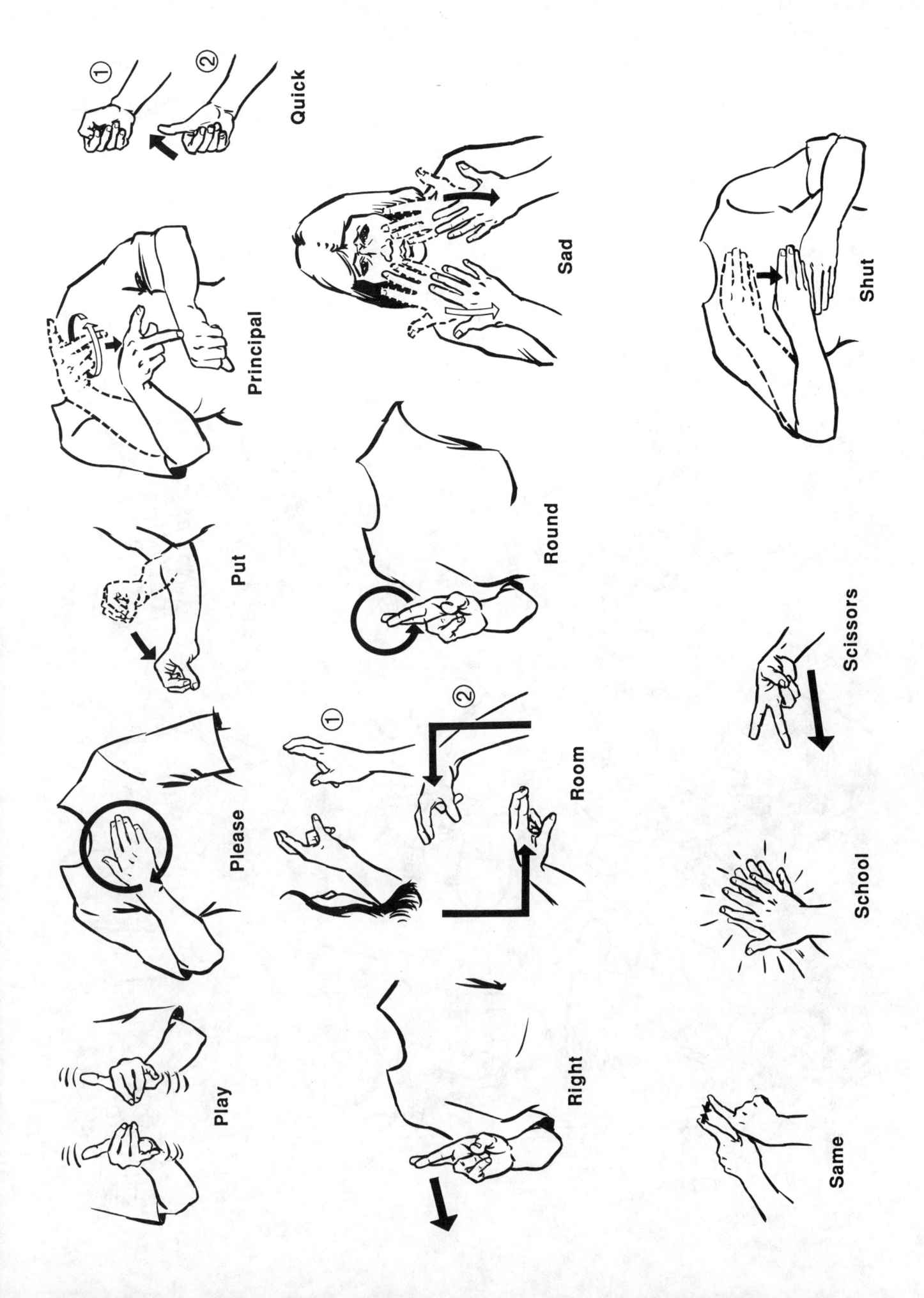

Put · Round · Scissors

Please · Room · School

Play · Right · Same

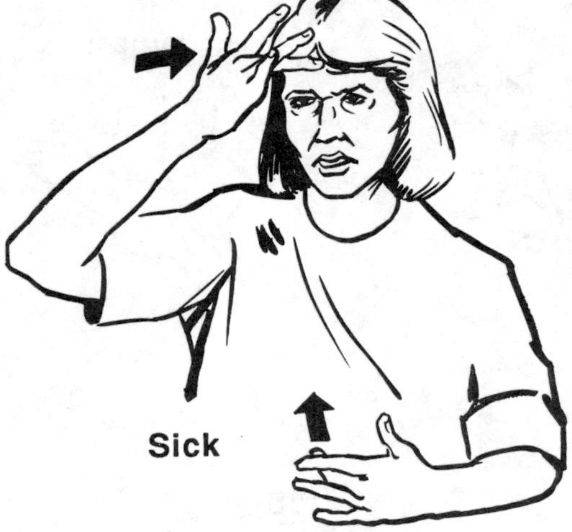

Sick

Sing

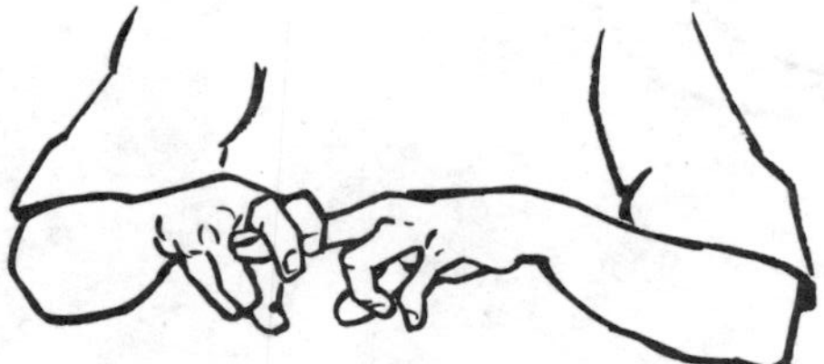

Sit

Slow

Sorry

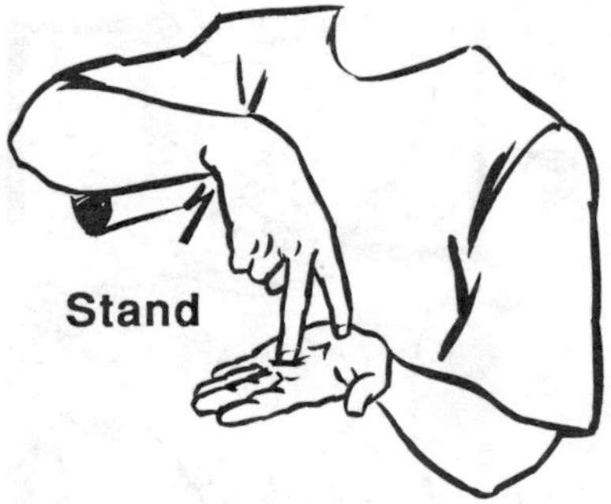

Stand

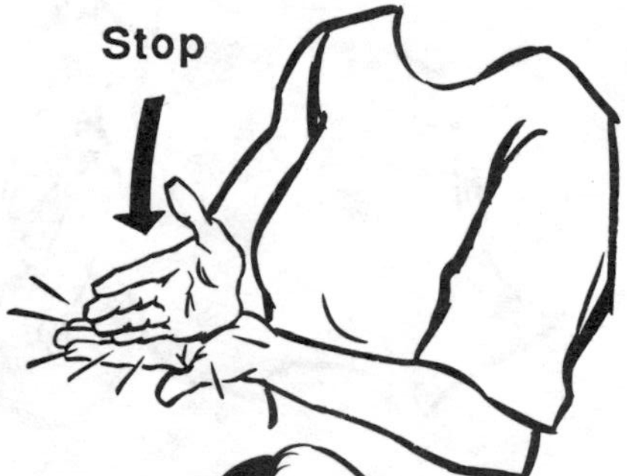

Stop

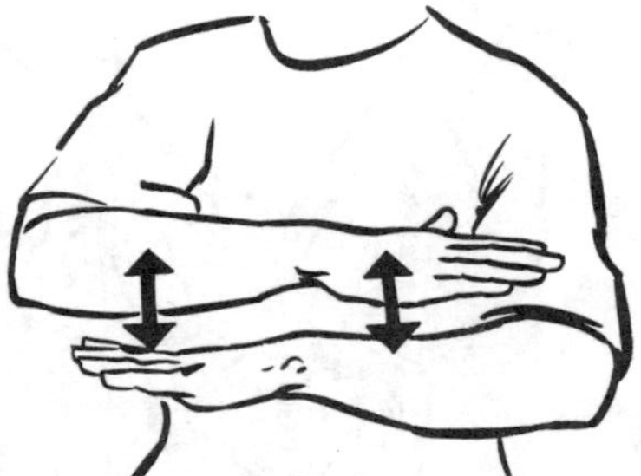

Table

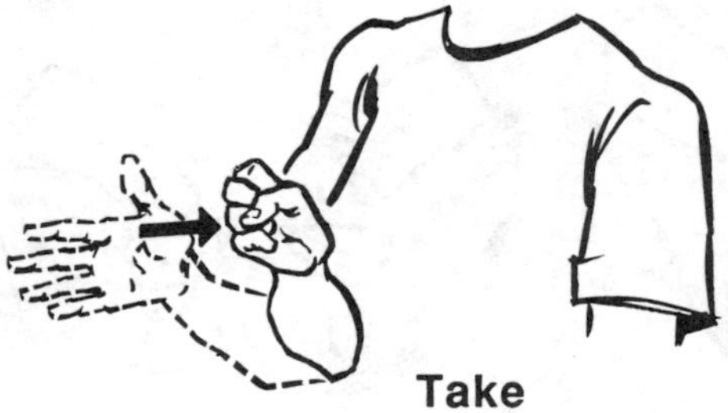

Take

Talk

Terrific

Thanks

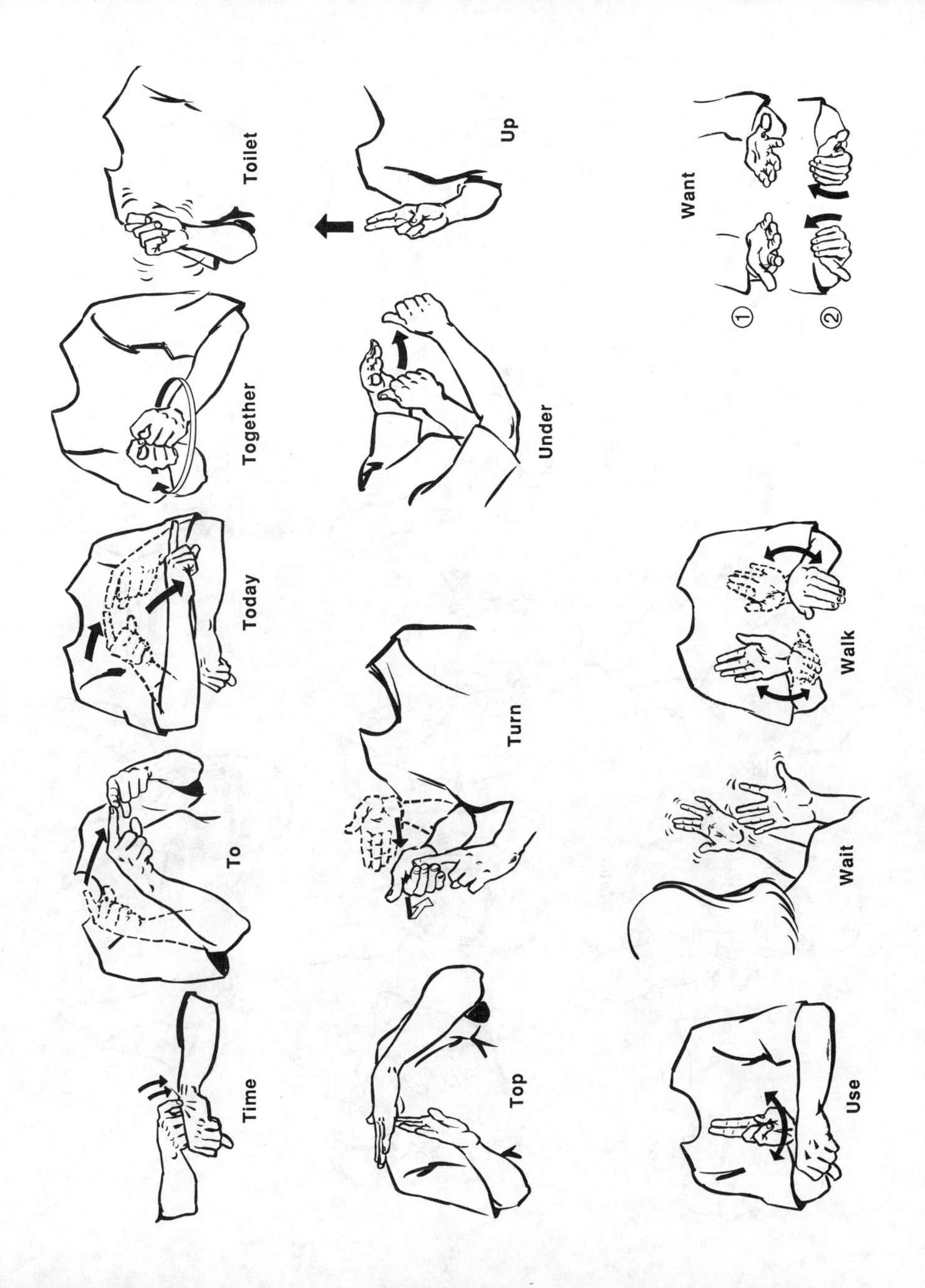

Time	To	Today	Together	Toilet
Top	Turn		Under	Up
Use	Wait	Walk		Want

Wash
Water
What
When
Where
Which
Who
Why
Word
Work
Write
Wrong
You
Your

Classroom Communication Lightbulbs

5

All of life is communication. We have five senses. People who have lost their hearing or their sight are usually considered handicapped. However, someone who has lost the sense of taste, smell, or touch feels equally handicapped. Sensory impairment is devastating. Imagine not being able to smell bread baking or brownies just out of the oven. Worse, imagine not being able to taste them! It is the combination of sensory stimuli that enhances the very essence of life itself.

PDD children are usually sensorily impaired in one or more areas. Our responsibility is to help them increase their awareness of the five senses. The senses are our primary defense mechanism. For example, visually impaired persons can still smell smoke, hear the flames crackling, feel the heat, and even taste the smoke as they try to breathe.

We have included touch, taste, and smell in this section on communication because vocabulary is inextricably intertwined with these senses. These three senses may elicit a much more positive response than do seeing and hearing. A PDD child who has been prenatally exposed to drugs will respond to these activities when nothing else seems to work. Looking at pictures of flowers isn't nearly as satisfying as picking and smelling them. Pictures of food don't taste good, but then again, they don't have calories, either. It follows that doing an activity—touching it, smelling it, mixing it— is far preferable to hearing about or even seeing it. These activities offer all children an opportunity to expand their knowledge through the use of touch, taste, and smell.

Although we have stressed the importance of the multimodality approach to teaching, the activities described in this chapter allow you the versatility needed to incorporate each sense independently or in concert with the others.

Touch, taste, and smell... These three senses may elicit a much more positive response than do seeing and hearing.

A. Can You Hear Me?

Auditory Discrimination

Auditory discrimination is the ability to hear sounds and know that there are differences in their meaning. For example, the child knows that *stop* is not *hop;* he or she won't hop when you say "stop." Here are some activities what will help improve any child's listening skills:

1. Present environmental sounds with pictures for the child to identify, (train picture with the sound of a whistle and choo-choo), then use the sounds without the picture.

2. Present loud and soft sounds (bang on your desk; tear paper).

3. Show two, three, or four pictures (place them face down). Play a corresponding sound and ask the child to choose the correct picture).

4. Give each child or group of children a special word. Each time the word is called, they have to stand up or clap their hands (use color words, animal names, foods, clothing, furniture, etc.). This can also be done when you are reciting a poem or telling a story.

5. Give the beginning sound of a special word. Tell the children to stand, eat an animal cracker, clap their hands, etc., when they hear another word that has the same sound at the beginning. For instance, the word is "boy," beginning with the sound "b." You say "apple, tree, bug." The correct thing for the children to do is to stand when they hear "bug." As the children master initial sounds, say "house, car, tub" and ask them which has "b" as the final sound.

6. Say two words such as "ball" and "tall." Ask the children if they are the same or different. Continue with a list, giving points, chips, etc. for correct answers.

7. Say two words such as "mess" and "less." Ask the children if these words rhyme. Continue giving points, etc., for correct answers.

Auditory Memory

Auditory memory is the ability to remember and utilize what is heard.

1. To the child say: "Say *baseball*." Let the child respond. "Now say it again but don't say *base*." Again wait for the response. The child should say "ball." Continue with a list of compound words or multisyllabic words. Later use sentences, omitting a word each time.

2. Have the child close his or her eyes. Using objects on the table, make several noises. Ask the child to replicate those noises in the same order (ring bell, tear paper, knock on wood, hit a drum).

3. Say three to seven associated words for the child to repeat in order. Begin with three words and add more when the child is successful. Say them slowly ("shirt, pants, socks, shoes, dress, belt").

4. Say three to seven unassociated words for the child to repeat in order. Say them slowly ("shoe, lock, apple, hammer, sun, swim").

5. Say three to seven numbers for the child to repeat in order. Numbers between one and ten are best ("1, 5, 8, 3").

6. Say a sentence; have the child repeat the sentence. Begin with short, simple ones and progress to longer, more difficult ones ("The sky is blue"; "The sky is blue with clouds," etc.).

7. Give one-, two-, three-, or maybe even four-step directions to see if the child can verbally repeat and physically follow them. Say them slowly, beginning with only one direction.

8. Say the Pledge of Allegiance, sing any song, or recite the same poem every day.

Auditory Closure

Auditory closure is the ability to combine sounds to say/read a word.

1. Break apart words into their individual sounds and ask the child "What's the word?" Use a one-second delay between each sound. For example, the word is "bug." Say "buh" (wait one second); say "uh" (one second); say "guh." "Is it good, bug, bag?" Then, as the child progresses, go to a two-second delay between each sound. When the skill is mastered, leave off the three clue words.

2. To the child say, "Say hot." Let the child respond. "Now say dog." Let the child respond. "Now put them together." The child should say "hot dog." Continue with a list of compound words or multisyllabic words.

Auditory Language Classification

Auditory language classification is the ability to classify, associate, group, and categorize information. It requires previous knowledge of the objects.

1. Name four objects (three that go together and one that does not). Have the child identify the noncategory item (*bunnies, kittens, cow, puppies*).

2. Name a category. Ask the child to name all the members. You can shorten allowable response time to help improve word retrieval speed. ("Name as many classmates as you can in ten seconds. Good! You got eight that time. Can you name them in eight seconds?")

3. Name four or five members of a category (*Ford, Toyota, Buick, Mazda*) and then let the child name the category. As the child is successful, reduce the number of category members you give as clues. Let the child name more. The next time name only three as clues.

4. Have the child tell how two named objects or situations are alike or different. ("How are a chair and footstool alike?" *They both have legs.* "How are they different?" *One is tall.*)

5. Use clues to help the child guess a secret object, place, person, or riddle. ("I know something that's tall, has branches, grows and you can climb it.")

6. Tell me an object you can use for _____ . (Insert action words: *jumping/rope; climbing/ladder*).

7. Listen to a word and name another word that begins with the same sound (*man, me, more, mad, mama*).

8. Let the child verbally indicate an acceptable response to an incomplete sentence ("For breakfast I ate_____.)

9. Make an absurd statement, let the child correct you and explain why it can't be right. ("An elephant watched TV with me last night!)

10. Tell the child a short story, then let him or her tell you the story back.

11. Ask detailed questions about a paragraph or story you just told.

B. I See You

Visual Discrimination

Visual discrimination is the ability to see and know that there are differences in words, people, places, and things. NOTE: Be aware, however, that PDD children may focus on details within a picture rather than the main item. Ask them why they answered as they did.

1. Show three or more objects. Let the children match same/different (three apples, one orange).

2. Let the children match objects that are almost the same (a green apple, a green apple with a stem, a red apple).

3. Let the children select matching items from a group of pictures (two spotted dogs, one cat).

4. Let the children match pictures that have the same characteristics (a red ball, a red car, a blue cube, a green pencil).

5. Let the children match objects or pictures of geometric forms.

6. Let the children match three-dimensional letters/numbers (wood, plastic, etc.)

7. Let the children match printed letters/numbers.

8. Let the children match printed words. Use flash cards, wipe on/wipe off, etc.

9. Let the children match words that are similar. Use some beginning sounds like *peel* and *peek*. You can also use ending sounds and middle sounds.

Visual Memory

Visual memory is the ability to remember and utilize what is seen.

1. Show a large animated street scene for ten to fifteen seconds. Turn the picture away and have the children name everything they saw.

2. Have the children close their eyes and tell everything placed on a table in the classroom, etc.

3. Show four or more objects/pictures. Have the children close their eyes. Take one or two away and let them name what is missing.

4. Show four or more objects/pictures. Have the children close their eyes. Take away all the objects, give back each object they can name.

5. Show the objects/pictures. Have the children close their eyes and add one or two more objects to the group. Can they tell you what has been added?

6. Show an object/picture and take it away. Have the children draw the object.

7. Have them describe everything they might see in their bedroom, in the cafeteria, library, or playground.

Visual Closure

Visual closure is the ability to understand the "whole picture" without seeing all of it.

1. Have the children put together a five-piece, twelve-piece, and then a fifteen-piece puzzle.

2. Have the children put together separated pieces to make a house, person, animal, (building blocks, geometric forms, etc.)

3. Give the children one-half of a picture. Let them draw the other half.

4. Show pictures with missing body parts or object parts. Let the children identify what's missing. Then let them draw in the missing parts.

5. Give them an alphabet or numeral dot-to-dot. See who can connect the dots and name the secret object/person/place.

6. Show a picture with a portion or portions covered. Can the children guess the hidden picture? This activity can be done gradually so that more and more is revealed (as in the television game show called *Concentration*).

Visual-Figure-Ground

Visual-figure-ground is the ability to pick out a specified object in a picture, scene, or photograph.

1. Play hide and go seek with just a little of the object showing (hide the pencil, leaving the point showing).

2. Use a "hidden picture" page and find objects named.

3. Use a picture containing hidden geometric figures. Find the shapes named.

4. Use a picture containing hidden letters or numbers. Find the letters or numbers named.

Visual Motor

Visual motor is the ability to see, then imitate an action. Lining up for lunch, picking up trays, and sitting at a desk are all visual motor skills that children practice regularly.

1. Ask the children to walk on a straight or crooked line placed on the floor.

2. Have the children imitate actions (running, jumping, catching, climbing) presented by peers.

3. Encourage the children to jump over a swinging rope or jump a turning rope.

4. Place two dots several feet apart on a chalkboard or bulletin board paper. Have the children draw a straight line between them.

5. Try to get the children to color within the lines.

6. Have the children cut out pictures of objects.

7. Show the children a geometric shape and let them draw one.

8. Show a letter or numeral. Let the children draw what they see.

9. Give the children a paper on which numerous shapes are printed. Draw one of the shapes on the chalkboard and ask the children to underline the matching shape on their paper. Then have them draw the same shape.

10. Have the children copy letters, numerals, or words from the chalkboard.

11. Have the children copy sentences or poems from the chalkboard.

Visual Language Classification

Visual language classification is the ability to classify/associate (group/categorize) what is seen.

1. Give the children a plastic bowl full of assorted objects (buttons, pegs, gym clips, coins, etc.). Have the students sort by category, color, shape, etc.

2. Let the children sort objects and tell how they are alike and different. As skills develop, do the same activity with pictures.

3. Put multiple objects on the floor or table. Let the children come up with ways that two or more could go together. These objects should be able to be grouped by several different characteristics. For example, put out at one time: a yellow umbrella, shoes, clothes hanger, grapefruit, coat, and apple. Possible groupings include the yellow umbrella/grapefruit, coat/hanger, apple/grapefruit.

4. Show a picture of several objects. Have the children help you make a list on the board of the different categories the objects might fit into.

5. Put out several objects or pictures and ask the children to point to an item you name.

6. Put out several objects or pictures. The children should name the object pointed to by the teacher or peer.

7. Place objects/pictures of varying colors, shapes, and sizes on the table. Have the child point to the "big block," then the "big red block."

8. Show objects/pictures that are related to a specific job (hose/firefighter). Have the children match them.

9. Show an object or a picture of an object and have the children explain where the object goes (picture of light bulb; they respond, "lamp").

10. Show an object or a picture of a object and let the children tell what other objects could go with it (baseball bat: ball, glove, playing field).

11. Show a picture of an action scene and then show a picture of an individual object. Ask the students if the item would be found in the action scene. For example, show a circus picture, then hold up a picture of a whale. Ask if it would be in the circus; why or why not?

12. Show absurd pictures. Have the children explain what is wrong and how they can make it right (child wearing a swimsuit in snow, making a snowman.)

13. Show after-the-event pictures (a girl in a cast). Ask what happened first.

14. Show objects or pictures and have the child identify the ones that begin or end with the same sound. As skills develop, ask about objects with the same middle sounds.

15. Give the students two or more three-dimensional or printed letters/numerals. Show the children a letter/numeral printed on a card and let them match the one shown with theirs.

16. Place alphabet strips on the children's desks. You can cover up portions initially, then expose all twenty-six letters. Hold up flashcards or letters for them to match on their strip. Decrease the amount of time each card is shown.

17. Give the children two or more simple printed words. Have the children match the printed model presented by the teacher.

18. Have the children write/print simple words from a model.

19. Give the children two or more simple printed words. Make a sound and ask the students to identify the word that begins with the same sound. As skills develop, ask them for words that have the same middle sound.

20. Give the children two or more printed words. Have the children write/print simple words which begin/end with the same sound as the model printed (model word is boat; they write bat or bit).

C. Touch Me!

1. Use "feely" boxes to teach identification of objects.

2. Use those same objects to discuss things that are hard, soft, bumpy, cold, hot, gooey, dry, slippery, wet, furry, rough, smooth, sharp, dull, etc.

3. Use a blindfold game to see if the children can guess who their fellow classmates are (from the waist up) or the identity of an object.

4. Simple physical education activities are great for improving coordination, balance, rhythm, extremity awareness, and spatial-temporal orientation.

5. Use slow symphonic music for rest time and during touch time for desensitization. Use pop music for partner/group dancing.

6. Have the children pick up small objects to sort; it improves eye-hand coordination, finger strength, and tactile control. (Put one small peg in place at a time.)

7. Make letters/numerals out of sandpaper, salt, or macaroni for the children to rub.

8. Other concepts related to physical qualities, such as thick-thin, heavy-light, can be taught by giving appropriate objects to the students and asking them to label the object.

9. Have the children close their eyes, hand them an object and let them describe it. Examples:

sandpaper (rough)	cotton ball (soft)
yarn ball (soft)	clay (soft)
board (smooth, hard)	fur (soft, smooth)
bark (rough, hard)	plastic cup (smooth)
nail (smooth, pointed)	upholstery (rough)
sea shell (cold, hard)	basket (rough, flexible)

10. Have the children finger paint and create pictures using various media: rice, salt, sand, beans, cornmeal, macaroni, instant pudding, shaving cream.

11. Make rubbings of objects (leaves, screen, fishnet, coins, paper clips, etc.). Use paper of various textures with chalk, pencil, or pastels.

12. Use hand and body motions for finger plays, poems, and songs.

D. That Smells Funny!

Since we are not olfactory scientists, we certainly cannot prove that a child's sense of smell is improving. We can, however, come up with some fun activities to emphasize the vocabulary associated with smells.

1. Acknowledge and ask students to identify everyday smells in the classroom: good, bad, rotten, fresh, sweet, sour, pungent, strong, dirty, clean.

2. Take a smelling walk through the school and decide if the smells are pleasant or unpleasant.

3. Any cooking activity is great for smells (popcorn, brownies, bread, cookies, fudge, etc.).

4. Bring in different kinds of flowers or bushes to compare.

5. Let the children smell the things they use every day (paper, hands, shoes, paint, their food, modeling dough, glue, the teacher, etc.).

6. Bring in different types of room fresheners and let the students vote on the one they want to remain in the classroom. (Take our advice and limit the number of days you use their choice so the smell won't get to you.)

7. Make a smelling center with empty perfume bottles, lotions, vinegar, rubbing alcohol, tissues, coffee, leather, rubber bands, cedar chips, newspaper, mint shampoo, cinnamon. Remember to check for toxicity.

E. It Tastes Yukky!

Just as with smell, we cannot judge if there is improvement in taste, but we can see improvement in vocabulary usage. So why not have fun with these activities? We can assure you that most misbehavior is reduced with this kind of stimulating lesson.

1. Come up with any activity where the kids get to taste, then judge for taste using the vocabulary associated with food: *sweet, sour, salty, bitter, hot, spicy, good, bad, peppery, cinnamon, soft, crunchy*, etc. Examples:

    popcorn(with or without salt)
    cinnamon toast (with or without sugar)
    crackers/pretzels (with or without salt)
    pickles (sweet/sour)
    chocolate (sweet/unsweetened)
    grapefruit juice (sweet/unsweetened)
    milk (whole/skim/chocolate)
    beans (cooked/uncooked)

2. Let the children cut and squeeze lemons to make lemonade. Put in all the ingredients except the sugar. Give each child a sip and talk about the taste. Add the sugar and enjoy.

3. Give each child a pinch of salt in one hand and pinch of sugar in the other. Have the child taste each one, then discuss the differences.

4. Put two textures together to taste (peanut butter on carrots).

5. Have the children do a complete cooking activity (making potato chips in the oven is great and easy, as is making peanut butter, pizzas, instant anything, milkshakes, gelatin, or butter). This list is only limited by your imagination.

Make sure none of your children has food allergies.

F. What Ya Gonna Do?

Don't Limit Your Themes

Whenever you present a new theme or concept to your children, there are a multitude of questions to be asked/answered. Each question fills in a little more information for the children and allows them to associate that information with the storehouse of knowledge they already possess. For example, here are some of the questions you could ask about animals. We've chosen to ask the questions about manatees (large water mammals), an endangered species.

1. What color are manatees?
2. What size are they?
3. How are they shaped?
4. How long are they or what is their height?
5. How wide are they?
6. How much do they weigh?
7. Are they fat or thin?
8. How many parts do they have?
9. What are the parts' names?
10. How do you use one?
11. Do they smell? (Do they smell funny or do they recognize scent?)
12. Where you do go to see them?
13. How often do you see them?
14. Do they feel hard or soft?
15. How fast can they swim?
16. How long do they live?
17. Are they dangerous to humans?
18. Can children touch them?
19. Are they like other kinds of animals?
20. What kind of animals live with them?
21. What category do they fit into?
22. What other animals fit into the same category?
23. Do they make noise?
24. Is it cold or hot where they live?
25. How many babies do they have?
26. What are the babies called?
27. What are adult female/male manatees called?
28. What do they eat?
29. How much do they eat?
30. What enemies do manatees have?
31. What kills the manatees?
32. How many manatees are left alive?
33. How can we protect the manatees?
34. What should you do if you see a manatee?
35. How can we adopt our very own manatee?

Just look at the language concepts you could teach just on this one theme, manatees. Teachers take for granted too often that a child understands a basic concept when in all actuality he or she might not understand it at all or may only understand the concept from one perspective. Just because a child says a lot of words does not mean that he or she has formed all the root connections necessary to grow a great tree of knowledge. Describing in minute detail is one way to help a child develop those minor interconnecting feeders.

Our example theme, manatees, can be incorporated in all subject areas: math, counting the manatees; reading, learning to identify all the words associated with manatees or writing a letter so the class could adopt a manatee; science, learning about how ecology affects the lives of manatees; social studies, learning about how to behave around manatees or why it is important that they stay alive; art, make a collage of different manatee pictures or make a stuffed manatee; music, see if the children can come up with words about manatees to go with a tune you have chosen.

We have chosen to use manatees as an example because they are a special interest of ours. If you would like to find out more about this endangered species, contact the Save the Manatee Club, 460 SR436, Suite 200, Casselberry, FL 32707.

Parents Are People Too

6

A. Parent/Caretaker Interview Guide

Parents of prenatally drug exposed children are not always the caregivers. If they are, communication and help from the home will more than likely be limited. In many instances a welfare agency will have custody of the child and/or the child may be in foster care or a group home. Sometimes, there are relatives, often grandparents, who are the child's caregivers. In all instances, communication and help from the home is vital.

Substance-addicted parents who are not recovering or being rehabilitated will be of little use in getting information or following up at home with intervention strategies. Use ingenuity in getting additional information by going to other relatives, health departments and involved agencies for help.

If the parents are recovering, please allow them the opportunity to help their child at home. Give them simple things to do, like asking them to sit on the steps with their child and point out the sky, trees, walkways, people, cars, etc. There are also preprinted calendars of activities for several grade levels available. If the system allows, ask willing parents to volunteer to help in the classroom. They can do so many things to help, but much more than that, they can learn so much from you and your students.

Always remember that the parents, not you, have the information about the child. Ask questions in a form that is not demeaning or invasive. By gentle probing, give the parents an opportunity to tell you what you need to know. Pushing them will most likely turn them off, and they will leave without having shared their observations with you. If you make the parents uncomfortable or defensive, chances are they will not follow through on any of your suggestions or instructions. Here are some helpful leading questions to ask:

1. What does _____ enjoy doing at home?
If the parent says "nothing," follow up with additional questions such as, "does he/she watch television, play with siblings, eat, color, like to be alone?" Keep asking until you get a response that you can label, even if it is "he likes to stare at the wall."

2. How does _____ entertain him/herself at home?
If the parent responds with "I don't know," follow up with examples. For instance, does he/she sing to himself, dance, bang with a hammer, stare at one object, fight, flap his/her arms, do the same thing over and over (perseverate)? Pursue until you get an answer.

> *Always remember that the parents, not you, have the information about the child.*

> *If you make the parents uncomfortable or defensive, chances are they will not follow through on any of your suggestions or instructions. Here are some helpful leading questions.*

89

3. What are some of the things that make _____ feel good/ happy at home?

If the parent response is "I don't know," ask leading questions to help find an answer: Does the child smile when you sing, laugh at television, act silly, play with you, ride a bicycle, eat ice cream, get new toys?

4. What have the doctors/professionals told you about what is wrong with _____?

If the parents give you a technical diagnosis, write it down and go to the next question. If their response is vague, ask if anyone else has been consulted about _____'s problem. Question them about any physical illness (measles, chicken pox, high fever, etc.) and shots.

5. Do you agree with their diagnosis?

Accept any response without asking for clarification. Go on to the next question.

6. If not, what do you think is wrong?

Accept any response without further questions.

7. What do you think _____ needs to learn to do at home?

If the parent responds, for example, "to clean his room," ask what exactly they want _____ to accomplish. Ask for specifics if their response is "just be good."

8. What have you tried to help _____ learn to do?

Accept any response and go to the next question.

9. Were you successful or not?

Accept any response without further questions.

10. If there are other children in the family, how do they act toward _____?

Try to encourage a detailed response, positive and/or negative. Ask for examples of incidents.

11. How do your other family members, both in and out of your household, feel about _____?

Encourage details, as in the previous question.

12. Are family members, or others, helping you tend to him/her?

Accept any response without further questions.

13. If you are in a store or shopping center and _____ throws him/herself on the floor and begins to scream, what do you do?

Accept any response without further questions or negative feedback.

14. How do you discipline_____ ?
Do not judge. Accept any response without asking for details.

15. How do you reward _____ ?
Do not judge. Accept any response.

16. Does it seem to work?

17. Do others in the family attempt to discipline_____ ?

18. How do they go about it?
Accept any response without question.

19. Describe how_____reacts to different members of your family (grandparents, siblings, cousins, etc.)

20. What would you liked to see changed about_____ ?
Encourage hopeful answers.

21. What would you like to see unchanged about_____ ?
Another way to ask this question is:
    What things about _____ are good?

22. What would you like to see_____learn to do this semester/quarter/year?
Accept any response. For example, if parents tell you they want their child to be a doctor or rocket scientist someday, don't laugh. Accept their statement with a nod.

23. Is there anything else, something special, that you feel is important for me to know in order to help your child?
Ask for clarification if you don't understand their statements.

91

B. Dealing With Parents' Frustration First

The old chicken or the egg argument can be applied to PDD children. The current predominant theory seems to be that a language/communication delay develops first, which causes the behavior/learning problems, which in turn cause the parenting stress. The following is a general progression of what may happen when a child is slow in developing speech/communication:

> 1. Child's language comprehension is slightly delayed.

> 2. Parents, siblings, and peers react by reducing stimulating interaction such as verbal expansions, imitations, questions, and nonverbal responses.

> 3. The reduced stimulation results in further developmental delays in language comprehension and verbal skills.

> 4. These further delays cause frustration for the parents, thus lowering their self-concept of their parenting skills, which they reflect onto the child.

> 5. The child now has a low self-concept and feeling of stress because of perceived nonacceptance; the child reacts with behavioral problems, acting in the belief that he or she is dumb or can't learn.

Parents of PDD children arrive at school having already been bombarded by well-intentioned family members and neighbors who have given them suggestions for improving their child's speech/behavior. These parents are resentful and hurt that their child is not normal and they have enough guilt to share with everybody.

When you are talking with them, please don't add any more "it's your fault" statements to assault their already diminished ego. At your first meeting, you need to get information from them by going over the Parent/Caretaker Interview Guide. Be honest and straightforward in answering their questions, but don't make any

Be honest and straightforward in answering their questions, but don't make any long-range predictions.

long-range predictions. Don't say that the child will be "normal" by the end of the school year, but you can assure them that the child will "improve." Be empathetic toward their frustrations and concerns no matter how you feel about their statements or questions. Parents need you to be as professional as possible, so please don't make condescending or authoritative responses. The more empathy and sincerity the parents perceive in you, the more apt they will be to give you information.

Always keep in mind that you, too, have biases about coping with and teaching these types of children. So try to be honest with yourself and with the parents about your own limitations. For example, teachers usually are not educationally equipped to handle deep-rooted family problems. Assist parents in setting up meetings with the school counselor or in getting help from area mental health facilities. Counseling can be beneficial for parents, PDD children, and their siblings. Not only do the handicapped children feel rejected, but siblings feel stress because of the extra attention given the "special one." Usually, the more impaired the child, the greater the stress on all family members.

Of course, not every parent of a child who exhibits learning problems needs intensive psychotherapy, but there could be some major emotional stresses that do not exist for parents of a "normal" child. We want you to understand that there could be more going on than just a child having learning and communication problems. Try to listen, give feedback, and reach out to other professionals immediately when you realize certain situations are beyond your expertise. Be like a lighthouse in a storm—the guide to help parents get closer to shore; the beacon that directs them to a safe port.

C. Promoting a Buy-in

You've now had one or more special children for a few weeks, and you have a pretty good idea about where they are developmentally. You have collected data to identify those behaviors that interfere with learning. It's time to ask the parents to come back for another meeting.

You want the parents' support. If they fail to follow through with the behavioral controls and educational objectives at home, your job can be twice as hard. When the parents arrive, you will need to go over all the information (developmental charts, behavioral data) with them. There are certain phrases that will boost your chances for a successful buy-in: "I need your help...," "Your child can achieve much more if we work together...," and "You are as important in your child's education as I am." These give parents a feeling of being necessary and important. Ask them if they agree with your evaluations and find out if they see anything different. It is okay to

Counseling can be beneficial for parents, PDD children, and their siblings.

have a difference of opinion, since that usually won't change your major objectives of modifying the child's behavior and increasing communication and learning.

Most parents respond better to a positive statement about their child. Try to use descriptions that include what the child does and has accomplished. Be honest and straightforward by giving information that is neither overly optimistic nor extremely pessimistic. Identify specific goals you want to achieve and describe how you are going to meet these goals. Tell the parents how you have structured your classroom, the rules the children must follow, and the consequences for inappropriate behavior. Explain the use of any items to control negative behavior (quiet chair, loss of privileges, checks, removal from the room, etc.). Then go over what happens if the child follows the rules (stickers, extra center time, treasure chest, etc.).

Encourage the parents to reinforce at home what is happening at school. Stress how important they are to the child's learning. If necessary, you can set up a system to notify parents about homework and behavior (positive and negative) on a daily basis either by report cards or telephone calls. Then at home the parents could go over the assignments, reward good behavior days, and punish off days (loss of television privileges, removal of toys). Just reach a mutually satisfactory agreement on any system that keeps you in continual contact with the parents.

Since young children initially need a great deal of reinforcement, you could tape the daily report card to their desks. For each hour of good, appropriate behavior, put a sticker on the card. If the child takes it home with five or six stickers, the parents will appreciate what a great day it has been. They can also have a behavior poster at home where the child can put stars or stickers earned. If he or she gets a predetermined number then the parent gives the child a reward or reinforcement, such as a movie, a pizza, or a trip to the park.

There are multiple ways to handle communication between the home and school. It doesn't matter what system you use as long as there is communication. The child must know that whatever happens at school, the adults at home will be informed. Hopefully, the parents and you will be partners in the decision-making process. The parents don't make specific educational choices, but when you choose the path, the parents can help keep the child from straying. Everyone, parents included, responds well to a pat on the back. If the parents/caretakers are even making an attempt to follow through at home, praise them. Reinforcement of positive behaviors cannot be overdone with children or their parents.

Most parents respond better to a positive statement about their child. Try to use descriptions that include what the child does and has accomplished.

Encourage the parents to reinforce at home what is happening at school. Stress how important they are to the child's learning.

Hodgepodge 7

A. Bandages

PDD children often find school, teachers, and other faculty members quite puzzling. We find the children alternately fascinating and maddening. They simply do not understand what makes us tick. We, on the other hand, cannot fathom why they won't sit down, be quiet, eat lunch, and play with their classmates. Don't try to figure out what makes these children go; there are no set answers, formulas, or whole books to read. PDD children just ARE, and WE are responsible for providing an education for them. Always try to bear in mind that they may not know how to behave. They must be taught–by you–to do nearly everything. Expect them to accomplish only a very small number of behaviors at a time. Many PDD children only successfully achieve improvement in one behavior during any given time frame. For this reason, it's often more effective to focus on one behavior at a time. Here are some techniques we've found useful in helping PDD children achieve acceptable school behavior and become ready to learn.

Always try to bear in mind that they may not know how to behave. They must be taught–by you–to do nearly everything.

1. Three Prong Approach

If you want the children to learn to put away the toys they play with at recess, don't just say "OK put your toys away." It won't work. You might try the three-prong approach we have found fairly successful:

1. Model putting away one object. Pick it up, saying "I am picking up toy." Put the toy in the proper place, saying "I am putting toy away." Repeat.

2. Put your hands over the child's hands. Pick up the toy with his or her hands "under" yours. (Make sure the child grasps the object. Close the child's fingers, if you must.) Repeat the same words again," _____, pick up toy." Use whatever reinforcer the PDD child responds to, and reward the behavior. (Tangible, immediate rewards generally work better than praise or hugs.) If the child even approximates the correct grasp, reinforce the behavior; this is called approximation. Move with the child (toy in his or her hand) to the shelf. While moving, say, "_____, put toy away." Using the child's hands, put the toy away. Reinforce.

3. Take another toy and again request that the child pick up the toy. If he or she does not, repeat steps one and two. Reinforce any approximation.

These three steps comprise a strategy known as *shaping*. It allows you to begin to shape the appropriate response.

Chaining, a related strategy, occurs when the child can put together the several tasks necessary to realize playtime is over, pick up the toy, and put it in the appropriate place. We have had children put the toy in the toilet—and be very proud to have put the toy away. They do not always understand "whys and wherefores." After all, you put paper in the toilet and flush it, don't you? Why shouldn't they put a toy they don't like in the toilet and flush it away? Both shaping and chaining can be very valuable educational strategies for PDD kids.

Approximation, on the other hand, can keep you from going stark, staring crazy! It enables you to live with the fact that PDD children cannot always string together even a few simple requests. Once you can accept this and not assume they are doing those horrible things just to upset you, life in the classroom will get better. We promise. Try to keep in mind that you didn't learn to water ski, ice skate, knit, use a lathe, or sew the very first time you tried. Remember— patience is a virtue.

2. Timers

What a wonderful invention a timer is! Buy a good one (it will cost from $8 to $15). The ones we use wind up. Plug-ins usually lose their effectiveness when a student pulls the electrical cord out of the socket or even right out of the timer.

Use the timer to indicate the end of one activity or to give a one-minute warning. Train the entire class to stop what they are doing when the timer goes off. Children adapt very quickly to artificial sounds that signal. Many PDD children don't respond to human voices very well and they will tune out your voice. They will however, hear the raucous ringing of a timer. It's important that you, as the teacher, stop the activity when the bell goes off. If you don't stop, why should your children stop? The kids quickly learn to pace themselves or time will run out. Your slow kids will be encouraged to speed up with their work and the fast kids to slow down with theirs. This, hopefully, will reduce the *I finished first* syndrome.

Timers may also be used for the quiet chair. Remember that a quiet chair is used to allow the child to get in control; it's not a punishment but a logical consequence for behavior. The suggested amount of quiet time is one minute for each year of age after the child has established self-control (i.e., five years old = five minutes).

> *Both shaping and chaining can be very valuable educational strategies for PDD kids.*

You will need two timers, obviously, if you want to use one for the quiet chair while another times a class activity. The kids will learn that any sound from the quiet chair area should be ignored.

Let the timer be your backup friend and not a source of stress. If you need more time, simply reset the clock before the bell buzzes and tell the children they have X amount of time to finish.

3. Classroom Management

1. Have colored disks on string for "getting into" the learning centers. Give each child a disk. (Yellow for music, blue for art, etc.) Have a peg, at each center. Two disks are allowed on each peg so the center doesn't get overcrowded.

2. Use bathroom "keys." When they are off the peg, someone is gone. When the "key" is returned someone else may go.

3. Post the class rules and have consequences for each rule. Go over the rules daily until the majority can readily tell you what each rule says, then once a week review all the rules. They bear repeating. Remind the students of the rules when the situation warrants. For example? "Rule #3 says 'raise your hand'." Thank those who remember to follow the rules.

4. When you move the class from one location to another don't stay at the front of the line. Have a student line leader so you can move up and down the line. Stop the group if they are disruptive, but don't yell. Remind them about hall etiquette.

4. Peer Involvement

Peer involvement is a powerful behavioral control tool, when used appropriately. Choose peer helpers carefully; watch for a few days before making a decision about which classmates "help" with the PDD students. Use these student helpers judiciously. Once they are chosen, it is easy to forget that they are young, too.

5. Consistency of Consequences

We cannot overstate the importance of limit setting and reinforcement. Make sure you are not reinforcing negative behaviors. When a teacher overtly gives attention to inappropriate (negative) behavior, this reaction unintentionally reinforces the probability of the negative behavior occurring again. It's better to downplay such reactions to negative behavior and expand, even exaggerate your responses to positive behavior. The reward system can be set up for one child, a small group, or an entire class.

Peer involvement is a powerful behavioral control tool, when used appropriately.

You can't overdo sincere praise. Encouragement breeds self-respect.

In late January or early February, you can attempt to initiate whole class peer pressure. You can reward a child or class for remaining on task for a specific length of time. The class can earn marbles, chips, or smiley faces for each predetermined segment of time that the particular behaviors do/don't occur. Set the number of chips, etc., to be earned before the entire class gets its reward (consequence) for positive behaviors. (Free time, videos, and extra learning center time are examples of positive consequences.) Try variations on this method; for example, you can take out one marble at a time until all are gone and the reward is lost. A check for each infraction of the rules is used by one teacher, and another class gives stars for good behavior. Do whatever you feel will work for your class. If you continue to have one or two students who will not/cannot follow the rules, then it would be time to go from group consequences back to individual consequences.

6. Praise

Use verbal praise profusely! Catch the students in the act of behaving appropriately. Praise, praise, praise! Reinforce, reinforce, reinforce! No matter what the semantics are in your situation, affirming a child and that child's appropriate behavior, response, or attitude can never be overdone. Encouragement breeds self-respect.

7. Touch, Touch, Touch

PDD children are tough to touch. Keep at it! Lightly touch the tops of their hands as you walk by; straighten a collar; tie a shoe then pat the foot. Never forget that while they need firmness, they also need affection, even if they don't know it yet.

8. Rewards

Have rewards every week or even every day. Consider designations such as "Boy of the week" and "Best sitter of the second row."

9. Signals

Use "signals" instead of words to calm them. Switch on/off lights, ring a bell, play a chord on the keyboard, or hold up a sign.

10. Stop-Start

While conducting a teacher-centered activity, use your talking to reduce the children's chatting. If they begin to whisper, immediately stop talking and look directly at the culprits. PDD kids need as little extraneous noise as possible, and it is good manners for every student to pay attention to the teacher.

Another way you can control behavior is to alter the rate and volume of your speech. If the class is very active and noisy, try giving verbal directions more slowly and softly. Let your body language mimic your slower rate of speech. Using a soft voice, move slowly around the room, incorporating exaggerated signing.

11. Limiting Movement

Getting children to remain seated and keep their hands to themselves is a thankless and frustrating task. Harnessing young children in their classroom seats is extremely controversial. Many educators look on a harness as little short of a straitjacket. However, with hyperactive children who have not developed their internal locus of control, PDD kids, and students who experience seizures, harnessing or a *Kinderchair* (see page 36) may be the safest solution. Some PDD kids are neurologically impaired and, as a result, have seizures and/or uncontrolled limb movement. Other PDD kids simply haven't been taught to sit still in their chairs. One of our students had been out of control during work time and at lunch for several weeks. We requested and received permission to harness the child during those times. It was amazing to watch the immediate change in behavior. The child welcomed the security the harness gave her. She even signed for it to be fastened. On-task behavior improved dramatically, lunch was eaten carefully, and academic skills became noticeably better. Do not discount the possibility that the children need the knowledge that they are being helped to maintain control.

Limiting movement becomes necessary only when children lose control or pose a threat to themselves or others. Any limiting of movement should be used sparingly and for **very short** periods of time (only until the child has regained control).

The safety of all the children is the issue any time movement is limited, regardless of the means or techniques.

B. Lollipops and Rainbows

An incredible array of reinforcers, motivators, and rewards is on the market today. Walk in any school supply house, variety store, craft shop, or bookstore and you will find an astonishing supply of items to purchase for positive, tangible reinforcers. Your imagination, however, will also assist you in coming up with lots of "freebies."

We have included in this section some of the reinforcers we have used, as well as some our colleagues have found to work. A word of caution is in order, however. If you use tangible reinforcers,

Primary reinforcers are considered to be anything tangible that someone can taste, touch, or smell, with heavy emphasis on the taste.

gradually phase them out and replace them with intangible reinforcers. Many PDD children will require a longer period of time than their "normal" classmates on tangible reinforcers (also called primary reinforcers) before you can begin to transition to intangibles. Use your own judgment about a time frame. You may want to utilize a behavior chart to record the child's behavior after a primary reinforcer has been given. Regularly chart the behavior and gradually add intangible reinforcers and phase out the tangible goodies.

Tangible (Primary) Reinforcers

popcorn	raisin toast
crackers	dry cereal
gelatin	carrot sticks
pudding	rice cakes
fruit juice	apples
frozen yogurt	oranges
sorbet	bananas
low fat milk	peanut butter
nuts	milkshakes
raisins	grapes

Of course, the list goes on and on. Just walk down the aisles of your favorite supermarket and you'll see many items that are tangible reinforcers. One of our nicest parents takes her child to the ice cream parlor before and after any event that takes place after the regular school day. It works. The kid performs like a champ, the parents are proud, and the child has passed another milestone toward normal developmental age.

Primary reinforcers are considered to be anything tangible that someone can taste, touch, or smell, with heavy emphasis on the taste. They are generally given "for keeps" to the students who earn them. Try to use nutritious and healthful reinforcers whenever possible. Transition away from food of any kind as quickly as is feasible.

Transitional Reinforcers

smell stickers	scented stamps
flowers	stuffed animal (to hold)
stars	medals (to wear)
ribbon (to wear)	badges (to wear)

Transitional reinforcers are probably the most important ones. After the children have pigged out on tangibles, we always hope they'll be ready for something they can see, but not eat. Two of our classes this year used neon-bright colored plastic visors as transitional reinforcers. The kids got to wear them when they earned a specific number of points for academic work completed and appropriate behavior. They didn't get to keep them until they had earned them for ten consecutive days. It was a thrill to see our middle graders around the campus proudly wearing fluorescent visors on their heads.

Intangible Reinforcers

points
award/certificate
pat on the back
teacher's errand runner
extra playtime
name on "good board"
hug
free time
no-homework pass
play with favorite toy
"that's great!"

The intangible reinforcers need to be customized for each child.

The intangible reinforcers need to be customized for each child. We have one child who would rather have a pat on the back than sixteen ice cream cones, and another who absolutely swoons when he gets a certificate. Ask the child what he or she prefers, or utilize your knowledge about each specific child to determine the best intangible reinforcer.

Miscellaneous Ideas

1. Treasure Chests—You can buy these commercially or make them up yourself. We have many fast food restaurants near our school, and they will almost always give us coupons, small prizes, and paper hats. Many banks, businesses, churches, and restaurants have key chains, pencils, pens, and balloons they will donate. You simply have to call them.

2. Time Shares—This reward takes only take a small amount of time and effort on your part. Offer an afternoon at the park, shopping mall, ice cream shop, or other special place as a reward for a job well done—behaviorally or academically. We never cease to be amazed at how much the children enjoy a little one-on-one. Many of our students come to one of our homes in a small country setting. They pick peaches at a local farm, come to our house and walk around the lake, pick blackberries, run, catch insects, pick flowers and just sit. We have a picnic and generally lie back and relax. Legal ramifications and/or school system rules may prevent you from engaging in time shares, however.

3. Display Cast-Offs—Our local department stores are often wonderful sources of unusual items they have used in displays. The cosmetic counters are especially fruitful because they change their displays regularly. We have gotten all sorts of items we can pass on to the kids just by asking to speak to store managers, explaining what we are looking for, and smiling hopefully into their faces.

4. Government Recreation Programs—Check into your town's recreation department, usually run by the local government. In our city we have an excellent department for special populations. During our school summer program, our children have gotten to swim, bowl, make pottery, play tennis (you should see the preschoolers do this), play on "big kids" playground equipment, sew, paint, and many other activities. Call them up; you may be surprised to see how excited they are to hear from you!

5. Films—Many libraries are discarding their 16-mm films because of the low cost and easy availability of videocassettes. We have acquired about three hundred films. Our staff is really excited about seeing the films that were produced in the 1950s, before many of them were born. You may even find some "oldie but goodie" television programs that everyone will love to watch. Expose all of your students to the popular culture of past decades.

There are so many possibilities to use for reinforcers, motivators, and enrichment. Young children have vivid imaginations. Crack kids, however, generally have to be led into using theirs. Always look for new and exciting things to introduce them to. They will expand their horizons only as far as you let them.

C. Collecting Data

You may bemoan the fact that throughout this book, we have urged you to collect data on each PDD child's behaviors. The forms in this book are, we believe, about the most basic ones we could devise that will still give you useful information. This information will give you a much better overall view of a child's strengths and weaknesses. Chart the behaviors, giving special attention to frequency, intensity, and duration. Try to determine why the child does certain things at certain times of the day. The time you spend focusing intently on the one child will help you plan a true communication/ behavior-enhancing classroom.

This same information can be utilized when you reach out to other staff members, including speech/language specialists, occupational therapists, special education teachers, school counselors, physical therapists, school nurses, school psychologists, and anyone else who can give you additional help.

Before you chart behavior, decide what information you need the most. Do you need to get an overall view of the child, or are you more interested in the frequency at which one or two behaviors occur?

The time you spend focusing intently on the one child will help you plan a true communication/ behavior-enhancing classroom.

For an overall view, make an ongoing list of everything the child does within a specific time frame (two hours, one school day), using the **Composite Behavior Form**. For the best data, compile your list over several days or even an entire week. Make sure you include positive and negative behaviors. See the completed sample form on page 104. The blackline master is at the back of the book.

Alternately you may choose to identify one or two behaviors that you will count each time they occur, using the **Behavior Frequency Form**. Choose the behaviors that irritate you the most. In some instances, you may want to record data daily or weekly until you can establish why some inappropriate behaviors are occurring with such frequency. Then take data every few months to see how much progress is being made. See the completed sample on page 105. The blackline master is at the back of the book.

We have provided several kinds of forms for you to use to help you analyze your PDD children, but others can be found in any good education textbook. Bookstores offer paperbacks that give you form after form to copy and use. Make up your own, adapt someone else's ideas, or use ours. Do, however, put down on paper the things that you learn about your crack kids. After you put the information down, study it and then develop a plan to help your PDD students grow physically, socially, and emotionally.

For the best data, compile your list over several days or even an entire week. Make sure you include positive and negative behaviors.

Composite Behavior Form

Name: Eugene
Observer: Kirkland
Date: 11-10/11-11/1991
Start Time: 10:06   Stop Time: 12:46

List *all* behaviors (appropriate and inappropriate) to get an overall view of the child.

1. hit Steven
2. jumped up/down in chair
3. screamed to play ball
4. ran away from room
5. rejected hug - cried
6. played beside Don - 5 mins.
7. threw milk carton
8. pushed Carlton in lunch line
9. ate crayon
10. watch 2 mins. of cartoon
11. swayed for 16 mins.
12. played alone at recess
13. colored all over page
14. could not sequence beads
15. talks in 3-4 word phrases
16. tore Maggie's picture
17. screamed while in quiet chair
18. wrote name with model (crooked)
19. could not group 2 categories
20. knocked over chair when not fir
21.
22.
23.
24.
25.
26.
27.
28.
29.
30.

From the behaviors listed identify those that need immediate change:

1. aggressive/violent behaviors (#'s 1, 2, 7, 8, 16, 20)
2. on-task behaviors (#'s 2, 4, 10)
3. academic skills acquisition (#'s 13, 14, 18, 19)
4.

* Use the *Behavior Frequency Form* as an additional diagnostic instrument.

Odom-Winn/Dunagan, 1991

Behavior Frequency Form

Name: Eugene Age: 5 9

(It is recommended that only one or two behaviors be charted during an observation. Take data regularly to see how much progress is being made.)

Date: 11-10-91
Behavior: Screaming
Start Time: 8:45 Stop Time: 9:15
Observer: Kirkland
Activity: "Good morning" time

Count circled: 38

Date: 11-11-91
Behavior: Out of chair
Start Time: 9:15 Stop Time: 9:30
Observer: Roberson
Activity: Story Circle

Count circled: 54

Date: 11-16-91
Behavior: Screaming
Start Time: 11:30 Stop Time: 12:00
Observer: Barnett
Activity: Recess - Free play + organized game

Count circled: 14

Date: 11-17-91
Behavior: Out of chair
Start Time: 10:00 Stop Time: 10:15
Observer: Dean
Activity: Music

Count circled: 3

Odom-Winn/Dunagan, 1991

D. Etcetera

We titled this chapter "Hodgepodge" because when we began to gather information (especially the kind that reposed in our heads), we hardly knew where to begin. There was no way to perfectly organize and write down all the things that we have tried in our classrooms.

In this book, we have not paid much attention to your other students. They have a right to be educated, too. Unfortunately, the overriding problems ("squeaky wheels") usually get the attention ("grease"). Your normal student population can help you teach appropriate lifestyles to your special kids, and they can benefit from the experience. Just remember that all children need many of the same things PDD kids need, just in different proportions.

Carve out a part of each day to pay special attention to a different child selected from your whole class. Call this child a Special Child, not a teacher's helper or pet. You could even call him or her King/Queen for a Day. On that child's day, plan some extra special treats: the child could join you for lunch, skip a hated assignment, or have some extra time in a favorite learning center. This is a day for some pampering, not running teacher's errands. Make it a reinforcing event.

PDD children will respond and grow. You must be ever vigilant, looking for new ideas to try, discarding the ones that don't work, building up the ones that do. These children did not ask to have the problems they have as they enter school. They have a right and we have a responsibility to provide as positive a start to their school days as possible.

Get to know your PDD kids inside out. Wear their personalities like a second skin. Get inside their heads. What can they do? How do they feel? What is their home life like? Do they have enough to eat? Is someone seeing that they are fed, bathed, and put to bed? Are their mothers still addicted? Why do these children sit so still one minute and jump out of their skin the next? Who are they?

Look for answers all the time. Ask everyone who could help. Don't be too proud to admit that you don't know everything. Go to the public library, talk to your family doctor, visit the health department or a residential drug rehabilitation center, see the movie *Rainman,* read magazine articles on children who are prenatally exposed to drugs, and then use all that knowledge. Couple the new knowledge with all your "old" skills, common sense, and a large dose of courage and perseverance, and set about educating these precious future-holders.

You may wonder why we keep harping on the same themes, albeit from various angles. The answer is simple. We are working every day with children whose eyes haunt us because they have seen things we hope never to see.

We have diverse backgrounds, but ended up in the same building working with identical student populations, so our methods, ideas, and teaching styles have been blended (maybe melted is a more appropriate choice of words) into this book. One of us is a very assertive, forceful, and take-charge kind of person. The other is...well, to put it kindly...a cream puff. So, as we have formulated the pages of this book, we have laughed, cried, fought, and cheered together, much as we did when we taught the same children. A city girl and a country girl certainly bring different outlooks to education. However, as we have written these pages, we have discovered that we are in total agreement about the one most important thing: **The child must be first.** For every teacher, petty disagreements, in-fighting among faculties, financial problems, personal crises, incompetent colleagues...all must take a back seat to the formidable task of really educating children. Crack kids will win your hearts. You will feel so helpless at times. Both of us have gone home and cried many tears after we've seen a child either make a tremendous giant step forward or fall into a deep hole of regression.

We wish we could sit down and talk one on one with each of you. Time and distance make that virtually impossible. We hope you will write to us and share your experiences, especially techniques you've used successfully, either yours or ours. These children's lives and futures are in your hands. Every step forward you help them take is one they do not have to take alone.

PERVASIVELY DEVELOPMENTALLY DELAYED CHARACTERISTICS CHECKLIST

NAME _____ DOB _____ DATE _____ TEACHER _____

CHECK ALL THAT APPLY:

COMMUNICATION
___ 1. inappropriately expresses needs
___ 2. little eye contact
___ 3. makes unusual sounds
___ 4. smiles rarely; almost never laughs
___ 5. flat affect
___ 6. trouble relating to people
___ 7. unintelligible (articulation errors)
___ 8. limited verbal responses
___ 9. echolalic
___ 10. abnormal speaking voice
___ 11. off topic responses

PHYSICAL/MOTOR SKILLS
___ 1. multiple health problems;
___ 2. extremely irritable
___ 3. extremely lethargic
___ 4. sensory disorientation
___ 5. unresponsive
___ 6. screams/cries without tears
___ 7. gross motor delays
___ 8. fine motor delays
___ 9. seems to be clumsy

BEHAVIOR
___ 1. ultrasensitive to stimulation
___ 2. self abusive
___ 3. doesn't handle routine changes
___ 4. self stimulation
___ 5. has ritualistic behaviors
___ 6. dislikes being touched
___ 7. poor transitioning skills
___ 8. behavior worsens in unstructured environment
___ 9. no consistency in behavior
___ 10. shows dislike/hostility to most
___ 11. aggressive
___ 12. temper tantrums and/or hysteria
___ 13. oppositional behavior
___ 14. seeming lack of fear
___ 15. shows no remorse
___ 16. hyperactive/impulsive

INTELLECTUAL
___ 1. impaired play skills
___ 2. poor object functionality
___ 3. attention deficits
___ 4. perseverative
___ 5. shows a preoccupation with objects
___ 6. poor spatial orientation
___ 7. academic problems
___ 8. phobias
___ 9. unable to sequence
___ 10. processing delays
___ 11. poor task organization
___ 12. language delays

Notes/Recommendations _____

Odom-Winn/Dunagan, 1991

Communication/Behavior Prompts

Name_____ Date_____ Evaluator_____

1. Say, "_____ come." What does the child do?
   _____

2. Put an object in a paper bag/box/purse. Look in it. Close it and shake it. Hold it out away from the child. What does the child do?
   _____

3. Put some food (snack/fruit) in a baby food jar, or blow some bubbles and put the wand back into the jar. Screw the lid down tightly. Put the jar in front of the child. What does the child do?
   _____

4. Roll a toy car to the child. What does the child do?
   _____

5. Exchange the car for a ball. Hand the ball to the child. What does the child do?
   _____

6. Wind up a toy. Let it "run down" on the table in front of the child. Hand the toy to the child if he/she doesn't take it. What does the child do?
   _____

7. Give the child a simple picture on a sheet of paper. Tell the child to color it, but DO NOT give a crayon. Hold the colors in your hand. What does the child do?
   _____

8. Give the child a piece of paper and crayons and say, "Draw a picture of you." What does the child do?
   _____

9. Hand the child a toy phone. Pick up your phone and say "HELLO." What does the child do?
   _____

10. Hold up two puppets. Ask, "Which one do you want?" If the child does not show a preference, just give the child one. Then say, "HELLO." What does the child do?
    _____

11. Begin reading and turning the pages in a book. What does the child do?
    _____

12. Give the child an 8-to-10 piece puzzle? What does the child do?
    _____

13. Ask, "Where's your _____" (eyes, hands, nose, feet, hair, ears, mouth, arms, legs, tummy). What does the child do?
    _____

14. Give the child five blocks to stack. If successful, give additional blocks one at a time up to ten. What does the child do?
    _____

15. Give the child a brush, comb, washcloth, toothbrush and a doll OR give a plate, spoon, cup, bowl, and a doll. What does the child do?
    _____

16. Give a set of rings and a pole. Say, "Stack them from largest to smallest." What does the child do?
    _____

Odom-Winn/Dunagan, 1991

DEVELOPMENTAL AGES CHECKLIST

NAME _____ DOB _____ DATE _____ TEACHER _____

INSTRUCTIONS: CHECK EACH BEHAVIOR THAT YOU FEEL THE CHILD EXHIBITS MORE THAN 50% OF THE TIME.

BY ONE YEAR

___ 1. Uses some gestures and sounds
___ 2. Uses consonant vowel combinations
___ 3. Uses some words
___ 4. Attempts to imitate oral sounds
___ 5. Responds to own name
___ 6. Vocalizes in a mirror
___ 7. Makes eye contact
___ 8. Quiets down when picked up
___ 9. Welcomes touching
___ 10. Responds to people differently
___ 11. Responds to facial expression
___ 12. Laughs at social play
___ 13. Smiles/giggles
___ 14. Entertains self for 5 minutes
___ 15. Drinks from a cup with assistance
___ 16. Picks up spoon by the handle
___ 17. Holds bottle
___ 18. Feeds self
___ 19. Waits patiently

BY TWO YEARS

___ 1. Uses multiple gestures and sounds
___ 2. Articulates h, p, b, m, n
___ 3. 20 words - 18 months
___ 4. 200-500 words - 24 months
___ 5. Uses words in combinations
___ 6. Uses words to direct attention
___ 7. Attempts to make self understood
___ 8. Attends for 3 minutes
___ 9. Refers to self by name
___ 10. Claims objects as "mine"
___ 11. Responds to "give me"
___ 12. Responds to praise
___ 13. Hugs, shows affection
___ 14. Plays by self for 10 minutes
___ 15. Rolls objects back and forth to another
___ 16. Indicates wet/soiled pants
___ 17. Drinks from cup
___ 18. Eats with a spoon
___ 19. Shares some
___ 20. Goes to specified location
___ 21. Follows two simple directions
___ 22. Matches based on color
___ 23. Groups objects by kind
___ 24. Identifies five body parts
___ 25. Names/points to pictures
___ 26. Turns two or three pages at a time
___ 27. Builds eight block tower
___ 28. Imitates gross/fine motor acts
___ 29. Uses objects correctly

BY THREE YEARS

___ 1. Articulates t, w, k, g, f, ng, y, d
___ 2. Vocabulary of 700-800 words
___ 3. 3-4 word combinations
___ 4. Uses some pronouns and adjectives
___ 5. Asks for distant objects
___ 6. Turn-takes in conversation
___ 7. Toileting completed
___ 8. Stacks five rings in order
___ 9. Walks up and down stairs alternating feet
___ 10. Complies with simple requests
___ 11. Talks for a doll/puppet
___ 12. Uses refusal to control
___ 13. Plays next to other children
___ 14. Attends with group 5-10 minutes
___ 15. Engages in simple make-believe
___ 16. Verbally indicates toileting needs
___ 17. Follows simple rules
___ 18. Stacks 9 block tower
___ 19. Strings large beads
___ 20. Folds paper with crease
___ 21. Turns pages singly
___ 22. Performs motions to songs
___ 23. Draws from a model
___ 24. Pays attention when being taught
___ 25. Interacts positively with peers
___ 26. Laughs at silly behavior
___ 27. Follows three step instructions
___ 28. Names primary colors
___ 29. Points out correct size
___ 30. Turns door knobs/lids
___ 31. Uses same objects for several purposes

Odom-Winn/Dunagan

DEVELOPMENTAL AGES CHECKLIST (con't)

BY FOUR YEARS

1. Articulates *r, s, sh, ch, th, l, v*
2. Speaks in complete sentences
3. 1500 word vocabulary
4. Places endings on words
5. Uses correct grammar
6. Uses articles and prepositions
7. Uses abstract words
8. Imitates 3-4 word phrases
9. Follows rules
10. Self-directed for 15 minutes
11. Attends with group 10 to 15 minutes
12. Attempts task before asking for help
13. Recites memorized sequences
14. Initiates peer contact/play
15. Says "please" and "thank you"
16. Expresses positive emotions
17. Talks briefly on the telephone
18. Shows sympathy
19. Uses imagination in play
20. Tells a plotless story
21. Carefully uses other's items
22. Distinguishes between fact/fantasy
23. Plays contentedly in a small group
24. Shows fondness
25. Buttons/unbuttons large buttons
26. Catches bouncing ball
27. Stands on foot 2-3 seconds
28. Matches circle, triangle, square
29. Strings small beads
30. Draws people with head, body, eyes

BY FIVE YEARS

1. Articulates *s, r, l* blends
2. 2000 word vocabulary
3. Uses adverbs and tenses
4. Uses all pronouns and articles
5. Uses eight word sentences
6. Plays turn-taking group games
7. Has a favorite friend
8. Reads numbers to 20 correctly
9. Answers telephone correctly
10. Listens to directions
11. Behaves in different situations
12. Expresses own feelings
13. Expresses how others feel
14. Asks for help
15. Skips on alternating feet
16. Kicks large moving ball
17. Bounces and catches ball in hands
18. Cuts along lines with scissors
19. Prints numbers and letters
20. Puts together 8-10 piece puzzle
21. Draws people with face, body, extremities
22. Tells story with a simple plot
23. Groups by category
24. Sequences by degree
25. Completes "what comes next" drawings
26. Understands alike and different
27. Makes suggestions
28. Persists at tasks
29. Rearranges objects in original sequence

Notes _____

DEVELOPMENTAL AGES CHECKLIST (con't)

BY FOUR YEARS

___ 1. Articulates *r, s, sh, ch, th, l, v*
___ 2. Speaks in complete sentences
___ 3. 1500 word vocabulary
___ 4. Places endings on words
___ 5. Uses correct grammar
___ 6. Uses articles and prepositions
___ 7. Uses abstract words
___ 8. Imitates 3-4 word phrases
___ 9. Follows rules
___ 10. Self-directed for 15 minutes
___ 11. Attends with group 10 to 15 minutes
___ 12. Attempts task before asking for help
___ 13. Recites memorized sequences
___ 14. Initiates peer contact/play
___ 15. Says "please" and "thank you"
___ 16. Expresses positive emotions
___ 17. Talks briefly on the telephone
___ 18. Shows sympathy
___ 19. Uses imagination in play
___ 20. Tells a plotless story
___ 21. Carefully uses other's items
___ 22. Distinguishes between fact/fantasy
___ 23. Plays contentedly in a small group
___ 24. Shows fondness
___ 25. Buttons/unbuttons large buttons
___ 26. Catches bouncing ball
___ 27. Stands on foot 2-3 seconds
___ 28. Matches circle, triangle, square
___ 29. Strings small beads
___ 30. Draws people with head, body, eyes

Notes _____

Odom-Winn/Dunagan, 1991

BY FIVE YEARS

___ 1. Articulates *s, r, l* blends
___ 2. 2000 word vocabulary
___ 3. Uses adverbs and tenses
___ 4. Uses all pronouns and articles
___ 5. Uses eight word sentences
___ 6. Plays turn-taking group games
___ 7. Has a favorite friend
___ 8. Reads numbers to 20 correctly
___ 9. Answers telephone correctly
___ 10. Listens to directions
___ 11. Behaves in different situations
___ 12. Expresses own feelings
___ 13. Expresses how others feel
___ 14. Asks for help
___ 15. Skips on alternating feet
___ 16. Kicks large moving ball
___ 17. Bounces and catches ball in hands
___ 18. Cuts along lines with scissors
___ 19. Prints numbers and letters
___ 20. Puts together 8-10 piece puzzle
___ 21. Draws people with face, body, extremities
___ 22. Tells story with a simple plot
___ 23. Groups by category
___ 24. Sequences by degree
___ 25. Completes "what comes next" drawings
___ 26. Understands alike and different
___ 27. Makes suggestions
___ 28. Persists at tasks
___ 29. Rearranges objects in original sequence

PERVASIVELY DEVELOPMENTALLY DELAYED CHARACTERISTICS CHECKLIST

CHECK ALL THAT APPLY:

COMMUNICATION
___ 1. inappropriately expresses needs
___ 2. little eye contact
___ 3. makes unusual sounds
___ 4. smiles rarely; almost never laughs
___ 5. flat affect
___ 6. trouble relating to people
___ 7. unintelligible (articulation errors)
___ 8. limited verbal responses
___ 9. echolalic
___ 10. abnormal speaking voice
___ 11. off topic responses

PHYSICAL/MOTOR SKILLS
___ 1. multiple health problems*
___ 2. extremely irritable
___ 3. extremely lethargic
___ 4. sensory disorientation
___ 5. unresponsive
___ 6. screams/cries without tears
___ 7. gross motor delays
___ 8. fine motor delays
___ 9. seems to be clumsy

BEHAVIOR
___ 1. ultrasensitive to stimulation
___ 2. self abusive
___ 3. doesn't handle routine changes
___ 4. self stimulation
___ 5. ritualistic behaviors
___ 6. dislikes being touched
___ 7. poor transitioning skills
___ 8. behavior worsens in unstructured environment
___ 9. no consistency in behavior
___ 10. shows dislike/hostility to most
___ 11. aggressive
___ 12. temper tantrums and/or hysteria
___ 13. oppositional behavior
___ 14. seeming lack of fear
___ 15. shows no remorse
___ 16. hyperactive/impulsivity

*List Multiple Health Problems and Other Notes_____

INTELLECTUAL
___ 1. impaired play skills
___ 2. poor object functionality
___ 3. attention deficits
___ 4. perseverative
___ 5. shows a preoccupation with objects
___ 6. poor spatial orientation
___ 7. academic problems
___ 8. phobias
___ 9. unable to sequence
___ 10. processing delays
___ 11. poor task organization
___ 12. language delays

Odom-Winn/Dunagan, 1991

Caretaker/Parent Interview Guide Form

Name_____ Date_____

Parent/Guardian_____ Interviewer_____

USE THIS AS A BASIC GUIDELINE FOR YOUR PARENT INTERVIEW

What does (child's name) enjoy doing at home?_____
_____
How does (child's name) entertain him/herself at home?_____
What are some of the things that make (child's name) feel good/happy at home?___
_____
What have the doctors/professionals told you about what is wrong with (child's name)?___
_____
Do you agree with their diagnosis? _____ If not, what do you think is wrong?___

What do you think (child's name) needs to learn to do at home?_____
_____
What have you tried to help (child's name) learn to do?_____
_____
Were you successful?_____
If there are other children in the family, how do they act toward (child's name)___
_____
How do your other family members both in and out of your household feel about (child's name)?___
_____
Are other family members helping you tend to (child's name)_____
If you are in the shopping center/store and (child's name) begins to fall on the floor, scream, and yell, what do you do?_____
_____
How do you discipline (child's name)?_____
_____
How do you reward (child's name)?_____
_____
Does it seem to work?_____
Do others in your family attempt to discipline (child's name)?_____
How do they go about it?_____
Describe how (child's name) reacts to different members of your family (grandparents, siblings, cousins, etc.)
_____
What would you like to see changed about (child's name)?_____
_____
What would you like to see unchanged about (child's name)?_____
_____
What would you like (child's name) to learn to do this semester/quarter/year?____
_____
Is there anything else (something special) that you feel is important for me to know in order to help (child's name)?_____
_____

Odom-Winn/Dunagan, 1991

Composite Behavior Form

Name_____ Date_____

Observer_____ Start Time_____ Stop Time_____

List *all* behaviors (appropriate and inappropriate) to get an overall view of the child.

1. _____   16. _____
2. _____   17. _____
3. _____   18. _____
4. _____   19. _____
5. _____   20. _____
6. _____   21. _____
7. _____   22. _____
8. _____   23. _____
9. _____   24. _____
10. _____   25. _____
11. _____   26. _____
12. _____   27. _____
13. _____   28. _____
14. _____   29. _____
15. _____   30. _____

From the behaviors listed identify those that need immediate change:

1. _____
2. _____
3. _____
4. _____

* Use the *Behavior Frequency Form* as an additional diagnostic instrument.

Behavior Frequency Form

Name_____ Age_____

(It is recommended that only one or two behaviors be charted during an observation. Take data regularly to see how much progress is being made.)

Date_____

Behavior_____

Start Time_____ Stop Time_____

Observer_____

Activity_____

5	10	15	20	25
30	35	40	45	50
55	60	65	70	75
80	85	90	95	100

Date_____

Behavior_____

Start Time_____ Stop Time_____

Observer_____

Activity_____

5	10	15	20	25
30	35	40	45	50
55	60	65	70	75
80	85	90	95	100

Date_____

Behavior_____

Start Time_____ Stop Time_____

Observer_____

Activity_____

5	10	15	20	25
30	35	40	45	50
55	60	65	70	75
80	85	90	95	100

Date_____

Behavior_____

Start Time_____ Stop Time_____

Observer_____

Activity_____

5	10	15	20	25
30	35	40	45	50
55	60	65	70	75
80	85	90	95	100

Odom-Winn/Dunagan, 1991

References

Brady, J. (1988, August 30), "Widespread abuse of drugs by pregnant women is found," *The New York Times*, Section C.

Brubakker, D.; Derouin, J.; and Morrison, H. (1980), *Treatment of Psychotic & Neurologically Impaired Children*. New York: Van Nostrand Reinhold Co.

Bunce, B. (1991), "Referential communication skills: guidelines for therapy," *Language, Speech, and Hearing Services in Schools*, Vol. 22, #1, pp. 296-301.

Calculator, S., et.al. (1983), "Evaluating the effectiveness of a communication board training program," *Journal of Speech and Hearing Disorders*, Vol. 48, pp. 185-191.

Camarata, S.; Hughes, C.; and Ruhl, K. (1988), "Mild/moderate behaviorally disordered students? A population at risk for language disorders," *Language, Speech, and Hearing Services in Schools*, Vol. 19, #2, pp. 191-200.

Canter, L. (1982), *Assertive Discipline*. Santa Monica, CA: Lee Canter & Associates, Inc.

Chaney, C. (1990), "Evaluating the whole language approach to language arts: the pros and cons," *Language, Speech, and Hearing Services in Schools*, Vol 21, #4, pp. 244-249.

Chasnoff, I. (1987, May), "Prenatal effects of cocaine," *Contemporary OB/GYN*, pp. 163-179.

Cooke, T., Editor (1981), *Early Independence: A Developmental Curriculum*. Bellvue, WA: Edmark Associates.

Dyson, A. (1988), "Phonetic inventories of 2 and 3 year old children," *Journal of Speech and Hearing Disorders*, Vol. 53, #1, pp. 89-93.

Goodman, K. (1986), *What's Whole in Whole Language?* Portsmouth, NH: Heineman.

Gruber, B. (1983), *Time Saving Tips for Teachers*. Palos Verdes, CA: Frank Schaffer Publications.

Jordan, R. and Powell, S. (1990), "Autism and the national curriculum," *British Journal of Special Education*, Vol. 17, #4, pp. 140-142.

Kantrowitz, B.; Wingert, P.; DeLaPena, N.; Gordon, J.; and Padgett, T. (1990, Feb.12),. "The crack children," *Newsweek*, pp. 62-63.

Kennedy, M.; Sheridan, M.; Radlinski,S.; and Beeghly, M. (1991), "Play-language relationships in young children with developmental delays: Implications for assessment," *Journal of Speech and Hearing Research*, Vol. 34, #1, pp. 112-123.

Kouri, T. (1989), "How manual sign acquisition relates to the development of spoken language: A case study," *Language, Speech, and Hearing Services in Schools*, Vol. 20, #1, pp. 50-62.

Kronstadt, D. (1989), *Pregnancy and Cocaine Addiction: An Overview of Impact and Treatment*. Sausalito, CA: Far West Laboratory for Educational Research and Development.

Lister, C. (1990),."The Piagetian method of critical exploration in understanding special education needs," *European Journal of Special Needs Education*, Vol. 5, #3, 176-186.

Maguire, J. (1990), *Care and Feeding of the Brain*. New York: Doubleday.

Mussen, P. et al (1969), *Child Development and Personality*. New York: Harper & Row.

National Association for the Education of Young Children (1991), *Position Statement of Developmentally Appropriate Practices in Programs for Four and Five year olds*.

Noisworth, J. et. al (1980), *Individualized Education for Preschool Children*. Maryland: Aspen Systems Co.

Norris, J. (1991), "Providing developmentally appropriate intervention to infants and young children with handicaps," *Topics in Early Childhood Special Education*, Vol. 11, pp. 21-35.

Norris, J. (1991). "Whole language-Applications to the Speech-Language Pathologists in the schools workshop," Unpublished Manuscript. Louisiana State University, Department of Communication Disorders.

Odom-Winn, D. & Steward, N. (1987). "A Screening Test of Anomia in Children-K, 1, 2," Unpublished manuscript and test.

Pascoe, E. (1991), "Can autism be cured?" *Woman's Day*, Vol. 3, pp. 50-53.

Peterson, N. (1987), *Early Intervention for Handicapped and At-Risk Children: An Introduction to Early Childhood-Special Education*. Denver: Love Publishing.

Prizant, B.; Audet, L.; Burke, G.; Hummel, L.; Maher, S.; and Theadore, G. (1990), "Communication disorders and emotionally/behavioral disorders in children and adolescents," *Journal of Speech and Hearing Disorders*, Vol. 55, #2, pp.179-192.

Rescorla, L. (1989), "The language development survey: A screening tool for delayed language in toddlers," *Journal Speech Hearing Disorders*, Vol. 54, #4, pp. 587-599.

Rollin,W. (1987), *The Psychology of Communication Disorders in Individuals and Their Families*. Englewood Cliffs, New Jersey: Prentice-Hall.

Scarborough, H. and Dobrich, W. (1990), "Development of children with early language delay," *Journal of Speech and Hearing Research*, Vol. 33, #2, pp. 70-83.

Schneider, J., Griffith,D., and Chasnoff, I. (1989). "Infants exposed to cocaine in utero; Implications for developmental assessment and intervention," *Infants and Young Children*, Vol. 2, #1, pp. 25-36.

Slenkovich, J.E. (1983), *94-142 As Applied to DSM III Diagnoses*. Cupertino, CA: Kinghorn Press.

State of Florida Department of Education. (1991, April). *School Age Hot Topics: Usable Research: Cocaine Babies-Educators Get Ready*. Tallahassee, FL.

Streissguth, A. and LaDue, R. (1985, Fall), "Psychological and behavioral effects in children prenatally exposed to alcohol," *Alcohol Health and Research World*, pp. 103-109.

Thal, D., Tobias, S. & Morrison, D. (1991), "Language and gesture in late talkers: A one -year follow up," *Journal of Speech and Hearing Research,* Vol. 34, #3, pp. 604-612.

Toufexis, A., with Cronin, M.; Ludke, M.; and Willwerth, J. (1991, May 13), "Crack Kids: Innocent Victims," *Time,* pp.56-60.

Weston, D.; Ivins, B.; Zuckerman, B.; Jones, C.; and Lopez, R. (1989), "Drug exposed babies–Research and clinical issues," *National Center for Clinical Infant Programs*,Vol. 9, #5, pp.89-95.

Wetherby, A. and Prizant, B. (1989), "The expression of communicative intent: Assessment guidelines," *Seminars in Speech and Language*, #10, pp. 77-91.

Yedle, J. (1986), *Second Language Development*. New York: The Magnetic Way.

Index

A

Acetylcholine 54
Aggression 35, 41-43
Aggressive behavior 41-43
  biting 42
  cursing 34
  fighting 41
  kicking 42
  hair pulling 41
  spitting 34, 43
  throwing 42
Aphasia 1, 4
Asperberger syndrome 1, 4
Auditory training 40, 76-79
  closure 78
  discrimination 76
  language classification 78-79
  memory 77
  ultrasensitivity 40
Autism 1, 4

B

Bathroom "keys" 97
Behavior(s) 41-43, 102-105
  aggressive 41-43
  composite behavior form 114
    explanation, instructions 103
    filled-out sample 104
  data collection 102-105
  difficulties 6
  frequency form 115
    explanation, instructions 103
    filled-out sample 105
  normal five-year-old 46, 105
  strategies for normalizing
    academic time 47
    inappropriate behavior 48-49
    music 34, 36, 47-48
    parallel play 47
    playground etiquette 46
    secrets 47
Behavior strategies
  buddy system 34
  in-seat 35-38
  modeling
    demonstrating 34
    speech 57-59
  on-task (Looking Up) 37-41
  restraint, physical 36, 99
    harness 36, 99
    Kinderchair 36

signals, hand 34
sitting down 33
Blocks 23, 80
Books 28-29
Brain 54
  corpus collosum 55
  hemispheres of 55
  neural pathways 54-56
  processes 54-56
  recuperative power of 55
  role in acquiring language 55
Brain damage 32
Buddy system 34

C

Caretaker/parent interview guide 113
  explanation, instruction 89-91
Caretakers 89-93
Chaining 96
Chronological age 33
Cocaine 54
  effect on emotional stability 54
Coloring skills 20
Communicate, How We 57
Communication, steps 56
  flow chart 57
Communication behavior prompts form 109
  explanation, instructions 9
  filled-out sample 11
Communication skills 31
  methods of improving 31
Communication, alternate forms 50
  communication boards 50
  computer-assisted voice synthesizer 50
  gestures 50
  sign language 50
  wallet pictures 50
Communication, reasons for 52
Concept Questions 87-88
Consequences 97-98
Consistency 37, 97-98
Control
  getting it 31-49
  praise for getting 22-23
Cooking activities 25
Counseling 93
Crack, definition 4, 54
  damage to child's brain 54

D

Data Collection 102-103
  behaviors 103, 105
  description of behavior 53
Desensitization 40-42
Desks 22-23
Developmental age 13-20
  by one year 13
  by two years 14
  by three years 14-15
  by four years 15-16
  by five years 16-17
  developmental ages checklist 110
    explanation, instructions 13-16
    filled-out sample 17
Developmental level 33
Drugs, effect on fetus 4, 54

E

Early Symptomalogy for Children (Prizant) 52
Emotional responses of PDD children 54
Equal and appropriate education 53
Expansion technique for speech improvement 58-59

F

Fears 2
Fetal Alcohol Syndrome 1
Functional level 31-32

G

Goodman (1986) 51

H

Harnesses 37, 99
Hyperactivity 2, 99

I

IDEA 32
Imagination activities 26-27

K

Kinderchair 36
Kudzu 56

119

L

Language, vocabulary concepts 2
    (See **Communication**)
Learning Centers 25-27, 97
    box center 25-26
    cooking corner 25
    imagination learning center 26-27
    pretend 26-27
    tea party 26
Lesson plan 20
Lines 97

M

Magazines 36
Perseverative behavior 36
Manatees 87-88
Manipulatives 24
    suppliers 24
Math 2, 25
Media Suppliers 27-28
Memory 54
    long term 54
    short term 54
Mental, emotional abnormalities 50
Modeling 95
Multisensory approach
    classroom instruction 60
Music 36, 47

N

Neurological impairment 54, 99

O

Olfactory training activities 85-86

P

Parent/School Cooperation 93-94
Parents
    interviews 31-32, 89-94
    support, involvement, 89-94
PDD, definition 1, 50
PDD characteristics 5-7, 108, 112
    behavior 6
    checklist 108, 112
        completed sample 8
        explanation, instructions 5-7
    communication 5
    intellectual 7
    physical motor 6

Peer involvement 97, 106
Pervasively developmentally
        delayed (PDD)
    definition 1, 4, 50
Physical/health problems 50
Plan, importance of having one 31
PL94-142 32
Praise 98
Prizant (1991) 52-53
Puzzles 80

Q

Questions to ask parents 89-92
Quiet chair 21-22, 34, 97

R

Reference books
    teaching strategies 27-28
Reinforcers 99-101
    customizing 101
    donations 101, 102
    food 100
    intangible 101
    tangible (primary) 44, 100
    transitional 100
Restraints 36, 99
Rewards 98, 106
Room set-up 21-23
Rules 3, 97
Running 2, 22

S

Screening instruments 30
    Battelle Developmental
            Inventory 29
    Brigance Inventories 29
    Burks Behavior Rating 29
    Early Language Milestone 29
Seating plans 22-23
Self-stimulating behaviors 43-44
    interventions 43-44
        distractions 44
        physical action 44
        replacement 44
        tangible reinforcement 44
Sensory training 75-88
Shaping 95-96
Signals 98
Signing 36, 60-74
Sitting down 33-35

intervention strategies 33-346
staying down 35-37
Skills 2
    fine motor 2
    gross motor 2
    verbal 50
Smell, sense of 40-41, 85-86
Social development 19-20, 32
Software suppliers 27-28
Sorting exercises 78-81, 83-86
Special education children in
        regular classrooms 53
    recommendation 53-54
Speech 58-59
    articulation 58
    expansion 59
    fluency 58
    voice differences 58
Speech and language delays 50
Speech improvement
    expansion technique 59
Substance addicted parents 89
Suppliers of materials 25-31

T

Tactile training 39, 40, 84-85
Tantrums 33, 52
Taste training 40-41, 86
Theme approach
    (whole language) 51
Timers 96-97
Touch training 39, 40, 84-85
Touching 40, 98

V

Verbal skills 50
Video Suppliers 27
Visual training 79-84
    closure 80-81
    discrimination 79-80
    figure-ground 81
    language classification 82-84
    memory 80
    motor 81-82
    ultrasensitivity 39

W

Whole language
        (theme approach) 51